Beyond the
BUNGALOW

House in Brighton, New York (Ca. 1925) (see Figure 185).

Beyond the
BUNGALOW

Grand Homes in the Arts & Crafts Tradition

PAUL DUCHSCHERER
Photography by Linda Svendsen

Gibbs Smith, Publisher
Salt Lake City

This book is dedicated to the preservation of America's historic architectural treasures, both large and small, which enrich our daily lives with pride, hope, and inspiration

First Edition
09 08 07 06 05 5 4 3 2 1

Published by
Gibbs Smith, Publisher
P.O. Box 667
Layton, Utah 84041

Orders: 1.800.748.5439
www.gibbs-smith.com

Designed by Dawn Sokol
Printed and bound in Hong Kong

Library of Congress Cataloging-in-Publication Data

Duchscherer, Paul.
    Beyond the bungalow : grand homes in the arts & crafts tradition / Paul
Duchscherer ; photographs by Linda Svendsen.—1st ed.
        p. cm.
    ISBN 1-58685-500-X
    1. Architecture, Domestic—United States.   2.   Arts and crafts
movement—Influence.   3.   Interior decoration—United States.   I. Title.

NA7571.D77 2005
728'.0973—dc22

2005010961

◈ CONTENTS

PREFACE

NOW WIDELY ACCLAIMED as America's favorite "Arts and Crafts Home," the bungalow is really part of an extended family that includes larger-scale homes. Some are near the bungalow in scale, while others are far beyond it. The purpose of this book is to encourage a new awareness of these larger-scale homes through a visual celebration of their remarkable artistic beauty, craftsmanship, and diversity of styles. Through striking examples taken from around the country, this book documents the wide influence of the Arts and Crafts movement and its strongest messenger, the Craftsman style. The book also explores the successive waves of other influences on popular architectural taste that mingled with the Craftsman style, creating design hybrids built on a larger-than-bungalow scale.

Although well deserved, the rediscovery and vast appeal of the American bungalow has tended to overshadow the charms and significance of other kinds of Arts and Crafts homes that just don't fit the bungalow mold. Largely fueled by endless promotion in specialty periodicals and through the raves of bungalow-centric books (this author's previous works included), the noisy celebration of all things bungalow is now into its second decade and doesn't seem to be quieting down. Meanwhile, less attention has been paid to larger-scale Arts and Crafts homes that comprise a range of crossover influences every bit as varied as any found in the

459:—TYPICAL RESIDENCE STREET, SEATTLE, WASH.

Figure 1.

POSTCARD SHOWING A "TYPICAL RESIDENCE STREET, SEATTLE, WASHINGTON." (CA. 1910).

Sited on a slight rise, a variety of larger Craftsman-style homes include two hipped-roof "American foursquares" (at far left, and third from left). In front of them, two children are visible in the planting strip along the curb. The other homes, also in the Craftsman style, have bungalow shapes but appear oversized. Because the coloring for such vintage postcards was applied by hand, it often resulted in floral displays (as seen here) that were more imaginary than documentary.

Figure 2.

HOME IN SPOKANE, WASHINGTON (CA. 1910).

Demurely peeking over a pair of colossal boulders of volcanic basalt (locally known as "haystack" outcroppings), this large two-story home in the historic South Hill neighborhood displays a rigidly symmetrical façade that is not typical of the Craftsman style. The sloping sides of its two dormers are also unusual. With site-specific serendipity, the entry stairs toward the front porch curve between the boulders. The stone's irregular pitted surface allows it to sustain a thriving rock garden. The backdrop of towering pines further hints at this region's natural beauty.

Figure 3. (below)

HOME IN SEATTLE, WASHINGTON (CA. 1915).

This larger-scale home in the Capitol Hill area was deliberately styled to appear modestly proportioned. Distinct variations in finish, color, and material designate each level, offsetting the building's considerable height with horizontal emphasis. Closer to the ground towards the right, an asymmetrical dip in the front gable's roof also helps to reduce the home's apparent size. While its style is predominantly Craftsman, the upper-gable peaks have English-inspired half-timbered detailing, a good example of a popular crossover style effect. On the original matching garage at left is a clipped (jerkin-headed) gable, a detail often linked to the English Cottage style, which seems to make an already diminutive structure appear even smaller.

Figure 4. (above)

"FOURPLEX" APARTMENT BUILDING, LOS ANGELES, CALIFORNIA (1913).

This example shows how successfully the Craftsman style could be applied to a multiunit structure. Well detailed throughout, the first floor is covered with horizontal clapboard siding. More delicately textured shingled walls denote the second floor, and a screen-backed lattice grid ventilates the attic. The front façade, with its prominently bracketed gable peak, recalls the Swiss Chalet style, further reinforced by the cutout design of the deck railing above the front porch. Because the building's massing resembles that of a large two-story house, it blends easily with the mostly single-family homes of its Angelino Heights neighborhood, a designated historic district. The area's variety of Victorian-era homes is a relative rarity in Los Angeles.

Figure 5. (right)

THE ALEXIS JEAN FOURNIER HOUSE, EAST AURORA, NEW YORK (1904).

Adjacent to the campus of the Roycroft Community, this home was once a barn, then remodeled into its present form by the Roycrofters and gifted to Fournier, the community's premier artist. His second-floor painting studio (on the left rear side) has a soaring ceiling and northerly light admitted through a sloping expanse of glass. The roofline and dormer, shingled walls, and stone details evoke the Craftsman style, but the house also includes elements of the Colonial Revival (classical porch columns) and Tudor Revival (half-timbering in the front gable). Sanctioned by community leader Elbert Hubbard, Tudor inspiration is consistent with the styles of various other Roycroft campus buildings. The dining room (seen in Figure 6) is at the right front corner and opens onto the front porch.

> The noisy celebration of all things bungalow
> is now into its second decade
> and doesn't seem to be quieting down.

"true bungalow" world. The sheer scope in variety of shapes and sizes represented among these larger homes entirely surpasses the widest range of the bungalow.

Although some non-bungalow homeowners may still feel left out of the hoopla, many owners of larger related homes would contend that theirs is as much an Arts and Crafts home as any bungalow. Some have gained this confidence by perusing the "family album" pages of *American Bungalow* magazine, where snapshots of larger Arts and Crafts homes sent in by readers often appear alongside photos of their smaller relatives. Many larger homes have also been the subjects of extensive editorial coverage in that and other current "old-house" periodicals (see Resources). Most are shown more for their unusual history, upgraded features, or furniture collections than for anything specific to their size, and from these it becomes tempting to generalize that every larger-scale home seems to have been built on a far bigger budget than any modest bungalow. However, this isn't always a given, as issues such as compact lot sizes and other planning factors that informed bungalow design were often the impetus for creating similarly economical designs for many two-story homes built across the country at the same time.

However, that argument diminishes in light of the famous oversized Arts and Crafts masterpieces created by the period's most famous architectural duo, Greene and Greene, whose choicest projects are cheekily dubbed "the ultimate bungalows." For many, however, the level of awe and reverence that such historic trophy homes elicit (particularly among devotees of Arts and Crafts design) has set an unrealistically high standard for evaluating almost all other larger homes of the period. Therefore, this book is intended to expand the perception of what constitutes an Arts and Crafts house (literally, beyond the bungalow). Thereby, the perception of Arts and Crafts homes as a clearly diverse, yet undeniably related group, will be further promoted and encouraged.

Any attempt to somehow define the relevance or importance of all larger Arts and Crafts homes by equating them with those that boast the finest architectural pedigree (or were built with the biggest budget) is misguided, and misses the point. Tangible or not, there are many other intriguing aspects to consider when evaluating the stature and integrity of any home. In these pages are examples to suit every taste and budget, and hopefully all will inspire. Savor the journey!

— PAUL DUCHSCHERER

Figure 6.

DINING ROOM DETAIL IN THE FOURNIER HOUSE.

Painted by Fournier, shifting light and color in an atmospheric landscape frieze called Times of the Day *encircles this room. Characteristic Craftsman-style features include the oak-beamed ceiling, high wainscot, plate rail for displaying small collectibles, and (at left) a built-in window seat beneath a row of south-facing windows with a garden view. The sideboard, an unusual Roycroft period piece, abuts the street-facing wall. Further to the right, an outside door opens onto the roomy front porch seen in Figure 5. Fournier painted another impressive landscape frieze of European scenes, carried out at a much larger scale for the perimeter of the Roycroft Inn lobby, which is still enjoyed by visitors and guests today.*

INTRODUCTION

Historic Overview: From Near to Far Beyond the Bungalow

MOST MAJOR AMERICAN CITIES experienced a burst of development in the early twentieth century, and almost all can boast entire neighborhoods of bungalows. Now historic housing stock, the bungalow's relatively youthful age has enhanced its likelihood of relatively intact survival. It also managed to stick around long enough to thrive once again as viable housing stock. But what of America's demand for larger housing during the same period? Most assuredly, such a demand was not only alive but also flourishing. In fact, the same forces that pushed bungalows into the forefront of the new housing market, such as the development of suburban tracts serviced by reliable public transportation, worked just as well to promote building larger-scale homes.

To understand what guided the public's demands concerning the exterior appearance, interior planning, and special features of most new housing at that time, one need look no further than the bungalow. Ironically, it was the modernity, practicality, and stylishness of the entire bungalow package that helped revise the standard of expectation for housing of all sizes and shapes for many years to come.

Despite the general bungalow mania, there were still plenty of middle-class people who remained unconvinced and would not make the bungalow commitment. There was more than a whiff of faddishness about its popularity. While this excited some, it didn't faze everyone and also made others hesitant. After all, for the entirety of the Victorian era and long before, single-story living was often associated with the mean, cramped cottages of lower-budget households, or perhaps something acceptable in an informal summer

Figure 7.

HOME IN DENVER, COLORADO (CA. 1915).

With a full-width, single-story porch that would look at home on a modest bungalow, this substantial brick Craftsman-style house also has a smaller side porch facing its driveway, which is lined with a border of mixed flowers in the manner of a cottage garden. The bracketed front eaves terminate in a clipped (jerkin-headed) gable sheltering an attic-level window. The gable's shape and the simple half-timbering effect on its face reflect two common English-derived elements that often crossed over into the Craftsman style. Although larger, this house has a similar orientation to the one seen in Figures 8 and 9.

Figure 8.

DESIGN FOR A HOUSE (1923).

Published in The Home, *an annual supplement for subscribers to the magazine* Women's Weekly, *this design accompanied an article called "Six Generous Rooms Without Waste," and attention was drawn to its economical yet stylish character. On a foundation of darker brick, the first floor's pale brick helps set off the single-story front porch. Exposed structural trusswork in its open gable, as well as the shingled gable and dormer configurations of the second floor, make simple Craftsman-style statements. Favorably compared to a bungalow, this design was specifically lauded for "the appearance of a story-and-a-half house," although its second floor provides just as much floor space as the first.*

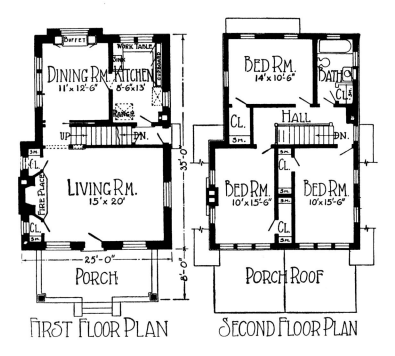

FIRST FLOOR PLAN   SECOND FLOOR PLAN

Figure 9.

FLOOR PLANS FOR HOUSE DESIGN IN FIGURE 8.

Strategically planned, this home's overall 25-foot width by 43-foot depth would allow it to fit on a fairly narrow and not particularly deep lot. While its layout offers square footage comparable to many one-story bungalows with similar amenities, it requires a considerably smaller footprint. As in many bungalow plans, the full-width living room is entered directly from the front porch and is well lit by windows on three sides. Doubling as circulation spaces, both the living room and dining room adjoin the stairway to the second floor; each primary room features the built-in cabinetry expected in Craftsman-style interiors. Next to the dining room, a compact kitchen adjoins a small vestibule for the basement stairs, and a secondary entrance on that side suggests an adjacent driveway.

cabin. Suddenly, it seemed that single-story living had been reinvented. With an artistic dash of style thrown in, the bungalow was a shining symbol of a middle-class respectability, and emblematic of a new era in the new century.

Even if it seemed to fit their needs, not every household identified with the bungalow's widely touted, egalitarian joys of living in such a simply conceived, modestly scaled dwelling. Some objected to the repetitive sameness of bungalow developments. Yet the bungalow's new reputation as a kind of treasure trove of all sorts of newfangled practical-planning arrangements and handy space-saving contrivances, quickly earned it a high profile. While not every bungalow may have deserved such acclaim, its celebrity sufficiently impressed the minds of Americans and helped raise the bar on their expectations from the housing industry. Henceforth, many of the so-called signature features originally associated with bungalows, such as opened-up living rooms and dining rooms, and built-ins such as sideboards, benches, desks, and even "disappearing beds," became quite commonplace in many other forms of American housing. These bungalow elements began appearing in the most compact and restrained of two-story designs (then nicknamed "bungaloid" homes), to duplexes and multiunit apartment buildings (SEE FIGURE 4), to far more grandly scaled homes that could realistically be considered mansions (SEE FIGURES 58–61, 66, 83–89, 124–28, 139–45, 163–74, 175–78).

When Is It (or Isn't It) a Bungalow?

There has long been confusion about which homes could or could not definitively be called a real or true bungalow. Some of this confusion still persists, usually among the more recently initiated housing buffs for whom an innocent misuse of that word is entirely forgivable. Official dictionary definitions reveal that the word *bungalow* is acknowledged to be an anglicized version of the Hindi word *bangala* (or *bangla*), used in reference to either the Bengal region of India or the indigenous mud-walled dwellings of that area. The original models (most rectangular in plan) featured high-pitched, thatched roofs with deep overhangs that created shady verandas encircling the buildings' perimeters. While most were small, some examples of *bangalas* had multiple rooms strung along both sides of a central hallway space that traversed the entirety of the structure, fostering better interior-air circulation.

These Bengalese dwellings came to be admired by resident British colonials for tempering the effects of the region's often scorching climate. By keeping the perimeter mud walls shaded and cool, a kind of passive ventilation system, especially effective at

Figure 10.

DESIGN FOR A HOUSE (1909).

The January issue of Gustav Stickley's The Craftsman *magazine featured this home in an article entitled "A Simple, Straightforward Design From Which Many Homes Have Been Built." It proclaimed this as one of their most popular plans. The magazine also pointed out that "although the illustration shows plastered walls and a foundation of fieldstone, the design lends itself quite as readily to walls of brick or stone, or even to shingles or clapboards, if a wooden house be desired." This home's overall form is almost severe in its simplicity, relieved only by the welcoming shed-roof porch, stone posts and chimneys, and the broad front gable with its deep eaves resting on exposed roof beams (purlins). Stickley's logo, in the form of a joiner's compass (at lower right), includes his adopted motto, "Als ik kan" (If I can).*

night, was created. The shape of the building's roof encouraged warm air to rise up and out through the roof's thatched peak, helping to draw cooler air into the house from the ground level. Early in their Indian occupation, the British coined the term *bungalow* to describe the colonial housing form they had loosely adapted from the original Bengalese model. Subsequently, there were various interpretations of bungalows built around the world, particularly in the tropical reaches of the empire, but by the time any bungalows appeared in Britain, little trace of their origins remained. In America, particularly in typical Craftsman-style bungalows, the large, sheltering roofs that cover front porches or create shade elsewhere with deeply over-hanging eaves are features that suggest an evolution from its Indian origins.

Most dictionaries further describe a bungalow as a "one- or one-and-a-half-story house with a porch or veranda," sounding somewhat vague and inconclusive. However, there is general agreement today that, by proper definition, bungalows must have most, if not all, bedrooms on the first floor, along with the other primary living spaces. This issue of bedroom location seems to persist as the most technically defining factor of a true bungalow. It should be noted that, by any home's mere outward appearance, confirmation of its bedroom locations isn't always apparent. In fact this may be completely imperceptible from the street, recalling the old adage that one can't judge a book by its cover (SEE FIGURES 12, 13, 43, 76, 108 AND 182).

Sources of the American Arts and Crafts Movement

Development of domestic architecture prior to the early twentieth century was characterized by successive waves of showy, historic revival styles. This taste for nostalgic eclecticism dominated American middle-class taste throughout most of the Victorian era. By 1900, change was already in the air. First, from inspirations generated within our own borders, important aspects of American architectural design reform were emerging and began to affect public taste. These included some groundbreaking residential work in the Shingle style and in the progressive style of the Prairie School associated with Frank Lloyd Wright. With these movements, the seeds of American modernism were being sown. Another influence that had a kind of cleansing effect on Victorian eclecticism was the Colonial Revival style. Widely embraced, its mantle of classical detailing and reference to nationalism helped it persist longer than other styles and ultimately outlast them all.

Another important factor was that by the late Victorian era, the level of education and professional training available to aspiring American architects was becoming far more comprehensive and sophisticated. Changes in building construction technology and engineering demanded this. Awareness and influence of international design trends (often acquired through trade journals such as *International Studio*) were also increasing. A movement away from the old apprentice system, sometimes driven more by working directly with the construction trade than by association with any architect, also marked the maturing of the architectural profession. These factors directly affected the work of American architects and became the driving force in turning the tide from freewheeling Victorian flights of fancy toward a more rational direction.

It was into this American scene, circa 1900, that the distinct influence of the

> With an artistic dash of style thrown in, the bungalow was a shining symbol of a middle-class respectability, and emblematic of a new era in the new century.

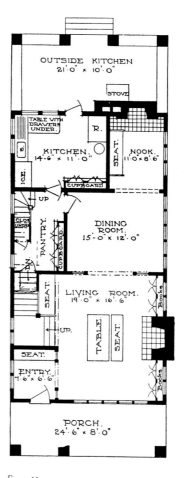
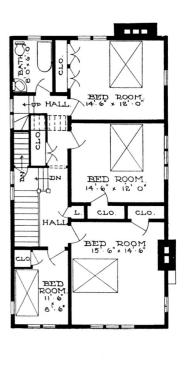

Figure 11.

FLOOR PLANS FOR HOUSE DESIGN IN FIGURE 10.

The first floor's interlocking sequence of spaces neatly divides public areas from utilitarian ones. To shield door drafts, heavy portières (doorway draperies) were advised for the entry's doorway to the living room, where built-in bookcases flank a large fireplace. While the rooms are not enormous, a feeling of spaciousness is induced by the diagonal view through the living and dining rooms and the nook at the far end, to a second fireplace. The dining room connects to a service pantry, then to either the basement or rear stairs intended for servant use. The outside kitchen on this plan was proposed only if it were built as a rural farmhouse, "as it affords outdoor place for such work as washing and ironing, canning, preserving and other tasks which are much less wearisome if done in the open air." A single shared second floor bathroom was common even in many larger homes of this period.

HOME IN SOUTH PASADENA, CALIFORNIA (CA. 1910).

With its swooping roofline descending to shelter its front porch, this full two-story Craftsman-style house was deliberately styled to resemble a smaller bungalow. To reduce its apparent mass and height, the forward-facing gable's roof is split as if it were a double dormer with interesting bracketing and stepped, vertical attic vents, but this actually covers the full width of the entire second floor. Over the front porch, the roof's angle conceals a large walk-out deck accessed from the front bedrooms. At the entry below, a cream-colored cat stands guard. The side driveway, a typical period feature, has a center strip of lawn intended to catch a car's oil drips, which would otherwise leave stains on a full-width concrete driveway. This home is quite comparable to the one in Figures 13 and 14.

Figure 13.

DESIGN FOR A HOUSE (CA. 1915).

Henry L. Wilson, a Los Angeles architect who called himself "The Bungalow Man," was also the publisher of numerous plan book designs such as this ("No. 400"). Appealing to public taste for the bungalow mode, he promoted this larger-scale plan as "a typical bungalow with all the low broad effect, and yet is practically a two-story house." He also claimed this design had already been built for $3,200 in the Los Angeles area "a score of times." In style, it mostly reflects the Craftsman taste, although a closer look reveals classically-inspired front-porch columns, and a Gothic-style motif in the quatrefoil (four-leaf-clover-shaped) cutouts of its railing. Some English Tudor–inspired half-timbering appears in the upper peaks of two forward-facing gables. While these seem to be a pair of dormers, they actually encompass the full width of the second floor (in a comparable way to the example seen in Figure 12). This is an effective device in reducing the impression of height and bulk in its two stories and in outwardly projecting a more modest sense of scale.

Arts and Crafts movement began appearing in domestic architecture and interiors. At first, it was seen in selected portions of higher-budget, architect-designed homes that were considered some of the cutting-edge projects of the moment. Starting as a design reform movement that originated in mid-nineteenth-century England, the Arts and Crafts movement's original intentions set out to improve public taste in general and the design quality and affordability of goods manufactured for home furnishings in particular. Soon, however, its influence in America would be galvanized into a recognizable design vocabulary, inspiring the creation of the Craftsman style that came to dominate the first wave of the emerging bungalow market.

More in England than ever in America, a central component to the Arts and Crafts movement was a preoccupation with improving perceived ills and inequities in both society at large and in the increasingly industrialized world. In pursuit of an idealistic dream that thrived only for a brief time, the movement's English leaders, most from privileged backgrounds, felt compelled to "save" unfortunate factory workers from a meaningless existence by helping them reinvent themselves as latter-day incarnations of medieval craftspeople. To encourage this, a number of so-called guilds were formed, with training opportunities for the willing to forge an honest yet creative living in fields involving traditional craft skills in the decorative arts, such as furniture making, bookbinding, weaving, metal work, glass work, ceramics, needlework, jewelry and ceramics. These were before models for similar ventures followed as part of America's Arts and Crafts movement, including the Roycroft, Byrdcliff, Rose Valley, and Arden communities.

America's Arts and Crafts Beginnings

William Morris (1834–1896), the movement's most famous English proponent, had attracted the attention of America's most progressive-minded intelligentsia long before 1900. While few truly embraced his agenda of socialism, some chose to decorate their homes with examples of handcrafted wallpapers, fabrics, furniture, and other signature decorative arts designed and produced under the auspices of his firm, Morris & Company. Some, such as Gustav Stickley (1858–1942) and Elbert Hubbard (1856–1915), made personal pilgrimages to England before 1900, and each would become famous as the movement's two most celebrated American proponents. Absorbing something of Morris and the movement's essence firsthand, each man came back highly impressed and deeply inspired. Both sought to develop appropriate ways to make a business out of reinterpreting at least some of the things Morris and others in his circle had been attempting to do.

Now, the Arts and Crafts movement took a uniquely American turn. While most of its lofty idealism (especially Morris' socialistic bent) met lukewarm receptions here, its elegantly spare aesthetics struck a timely chord, and the canny American sense of a business opportunity began to develop around it. What did survive from England, however, was the movement's basic tenet of design restraint, using honest natural materials as well as forms appropriate to a specified function, whether applied to objects, furniture, interiors, or entire buildings. Armed with their personal reinventions of the original Arts and Crafts movement, Stickley and Hubbard were able to convince many others of its validity and great potential in a specialized home furnishings market. The work of each would soon become a broader influence in the fields of interior and domestic architectural design. Stickley and Hubbard each became one of the remarkable success stories of their day.

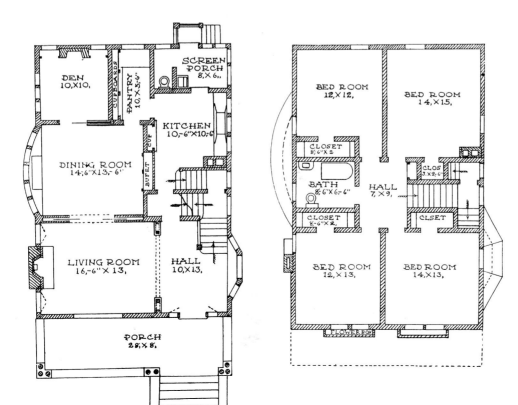

Figure 14.

FLOOR PLANS FOR HOUSE DESIGN IN FIGURE 13.

Continuing the impression of its exterior, this home's first-floor plan has features in common with many smaller bungalows. To make it feel more spacious, the entry hall with the staircase in view is open to the living room and separated only by a wide opening with a colonnade. Reinforcing this spatial connection, the entry's angled bay window is on an axis with the living room fireplace. In a similar way as seen in Figure 11, the sequences of public spaces are connected through wide doorways with pocket doors, creating a long vista terminating with a second fireplace in the den. Dining room built-ins include a buffet and room-wide window seat in a bow-shaped bay. A service stair rises from the kitchen, but connects back to the main staircase at a mid-floor landing. On the second floor, a central stair hall opens to the bathroom and to four nearly equal bedrooms in each corner; all have windows on two sides.

Figure 15.

TWO VIEWS OF A HOUSE DESIGN (1909).

Published in the January issue of The Craftsman, *this home was described in an article headlined "House With Court, Pergolas, Outdoor Living Rooms, and Sleeping Balconies." Though beyond a bungalow in scale and plan, its design utilizes many Craftsman-style elements. The article stated, "Such a plan would serve admirably for a dwelling in California or in the Southern States, but would be advisable only for specially favored spots in the North and East, as its comfort and charm necessarily depend very largely upon the possibility of outdoor life." Building materials include stone foundation and chimneys, cement (or stucco) on the first floor, wood shingles on the upper walls, and a red tile roof. Gustav Stickley's logo (with his motto) appears in the lower-left corner of each drawing.*

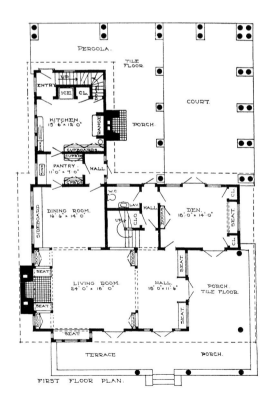 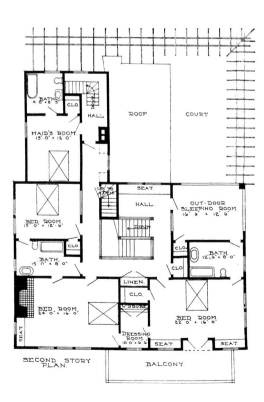

Figure 16.

FLOOR PLANS FOR HOUSE DESIGN IN FIGURE 15.

While not exceptionally large in square footage, this design's extensive outdoor living areas double the usable living space of its first floor. An open front-terrace porch with a low stone railing wall leads to the entry hall, where french doors open to a large covered porch. Both the main staircase and dining room, except for their colonnades, are open to the entry and living room. An inglenook with typical built-ins anchors the living room. Off the entry is a generous den with more built-ins, and french doors opening to both the covered porch and rear open court area. Past the stairs and off a short hall is the guest bathroom and a door to a covered rear porch, where an outside fireplace shares its chimney with the kitchen range.

ELBERT HUBBARD
AND THE ROYCROFT COMMUNITY

By 1895, Elbert Hubbard (1856-1915), a retired, well-to-do businessman with a strong sales background gained with the Larkin Soap Company in Buffalo, had founded the Roycroft community in nearby East Aurora, New York, on the inspiration of his investigative foray into England's Arts and Crafts world (SEE FIGURES 5 AND 6). At its peak, Roycroft employed over 500 workers. Of all the so-called "utopian" craft communities inspired by those of England's Arts and Crafts movement, the Roycroft was by far the most successful. However, in its actual administration, it was more of a benevolent dictatorship than a true utopian operation.

Hubbard managed a thriving community of craftspeople who produced a wide range of decorative arts, from metalwork to leatherwork and bookbinding to furniture. Locally generated sales, coupled with a thriving mail-order business, provided lucrative venues from which Hubbard was able to hawk his community's famously handcrafted merchandise. A self-styled, folksy philosopher of sorts, he also vented his opinionated views through active participation in the lecture circuit, in various Roycroft-published books, and in periodicals—including the *Fra* and the *Philistine*. After his premature death in 1915, when he and his wife, Alice, drowned in the sinking of the Lusitania, the leadership of the enterprise was taken over by his son Elbert Hubbard II, called "Bert" (SEE FIGURES 175-78). It survived several ups and downs, but closed in 1938. Today, the Roycroft is once again a flourishing community of artists and craftspeople, working in and around its East Aurora campus. In addition to those locally based, there are a number of officially sanctioned Roycroft Renaissance artisans working elsewhere around the country. Hubbard's beloved enclave of stone and half-timbered buildings survives as a testament to his English Arts and Crafts inspiration, and remains an important site for Arts and Crafts devotees of today. As they have since it first opened in 1905, guests of the Roycroft Inn can settle into atmospheric period-style lodgings, partake of food and Hubbard-style good cheer, and explore the Roycroft campus, the village of East Aurora, the important architectural landmarks of Buffalo, and the historic Niagara frontier.

Catalog Homes: Plan Book Designs

In his time, Stickley's was a relatively small part of America's house-plan business; it had already been firmly established during the Victorian era. As the economy boomed in the early twentieth century and the need for housing of all types escalated rapidly, many others besides Stickley quickly seized the opportunity to jump on the housing bandwagon. Although not a new idea, the concept of plan books—catalogs of house designs and their floor plans—figured strongly in the development of new housing in the bungalow era. While plan books certainly fueled much interest in those compact wonders, many offered an expanded selection, including a variety of two-story house-plan choices ranging from extremely simple to relatively grand (SEE FIGURES 13–16, 80, 107, 118, 129, 146 AND 179).

For many prospective individual homeowners, the plan book route made the selection of a dream house a near-seamless experience of armchair shopping. While plan books were inexpensive or free and very easy to obtain, their various publishers profited from the sales of complete sets of working drawings sufficient for construction purposes. Most of these plan sets were sold for between five and twenty-five dollars. Still to be incurred, however, were the expenses of a suitable building lot as well as the labor and material costs generated by the building contractor. Driven by location and demand, land costs were the greatest variable.

Much to the chagrin of the architectural profession, the exceptional popularity of the plan book process circumvented the need for most people to hire an architect to design their home. Many large housing tracts were built by ambitious real estate developers using only plan book home designs. Ironically, plan book businesses were also the gainful employers of the services of some professional architects, as well as talented draftsmen with architectural experience but often without formal training. Unfortunately, plan book designs were frequently published without giving credit to their specific designer, so the significant talents evidenced in many of those homes remain anonymous. However, because architectural firms usually did receive proper credit for any work featured in professional trade journals or periodicals, the creative forces behind other important period designs have thus been identified by later research.

GUSTAV STICKLEY
AND THE CRAFTSMAN EMPIRE

Gustav Stickley (1858–1942), an energetic man from a modest background, was trained as a stonemason, metalworker, and furniture maker. He came from a large family, and had several siblings who also went into the furniture business separately. The impressions that Stickley gathered of the English Arts and Crafts movement and its proponents on his trip to England in 1898 greatly inspired his own creation of a successful business empire. Soon after returning from England, he opened his own furniture workshop in Eastwood, New York, called United Crafts, which he expanded and renamed the Craftsman Workshops in 1900. Stickley developed his signature "Craftsman" line of spare, sturdy furniture designs, utilizing simple but high-quality materials and employing solid, traditional joinery techniques. As the business grew, he eventually expanded his offerings to include other decorative arts, such as lighting fixtures, metalwork, and textiles—all designed to complement the aesthetics of his furniture.

Like Elbert Hubbard, he also created his own periodical, the *Craftsman* magazine, which further elevated his standing as an influential tastemaker. However, Stickley departed from what Hubbard was doing when he began to market designs and building plans for new Craftsman homes that embodied his personal vision of the ideal American home. As much as his furnishings, these homes were inspired by his interpretation of Arts and Crafts design principles, and helped escalate the popularity of the Craftsman style to an ever-widening audience. Prophetically, he was among the earliest and most vocal in lauding the modest bungalow as the ideal embodiment of a simple American home.

While they were a key aspect of the so-called "Craftsman way of life" that Stickley obsessively encouraged, bungalows weren't the only kind of homes he endorsed and marketed. In the years of its publication, between 1901 and 1916, his magazine presented many new Craftsman home designs and plans, and a variety of larger two-story designs were included, many with bungalow-style amenities (SEE FIGURES 10, 11, 15, 16 AND 27). In its mix of articles and editorial advice, *The Craftsman* also covered progressively designed homes by others, including the work of Greene and Greene. Although national circulation of *The Craftsman* didn't come close to that of its competition, the major national periodicals such as *House Beautiful, House & Garden,* or *Ladies' Home Journal,* it managed to exert some influence over the type of homes and styles these magazines covered, thus more widely affecting the perception and direction of middle-class taste.

Although Stickley's Craftsman homes exerted a nationwide influence on the building industry, his prominence would actually work against him. From an early date, unscrupulous competitors wanting a piece of his lucrative pie routinely bootlegged his house and furniture designs. The relatively high visibility of Stickley's published efforts (and those of Hubbard as well) also tended to foster the assimilation of an Arts and Crafts sensibility into mainstream public taste, which after a time took on its own momentum without them. Stickley's own Craftsman brand name became a familiar household word. After the bankruptcy of his business in 1916, a victim of overzealous mismanagement, homes and furnishings by others that imitated or adapted his style also propelled his Craftsman name further into generic nomenclature, where it persists to this day.

The Kit House Phenomenon

Most famously launched by Sears, Roebuck and Company by 1909, a remarkably innovative industry made it possible to purchase a home selected from a catalog. Kit houses (sometimes also called "Ready-cut") arrived in the form of stacked lumber for structural framing, and in various other prefabricated parts (SEE FIGURE 17). These were shipped on pallets to the nearest city or town, then trucked to the new home's specified location, and assembled by a local contractor or a particularly handy homeowner. Precut structural lumber, interior moldings and trim, window and doorframes, and built-in cabinetry were all carefully numbered according to plans that guided their assembly. Soon after Sears had taken the lead, competition from rivals like Montgomery Ward appeared. Usually located in lumber-rich areas, there were also a number of other firms—such as Aladdin Homes of Bay City, Michigan, and Gordon-Van Tine Company of Davenport, Iowa—who made the production of kit homes their specialty. The kit house phenomenon was far more prevalent than most people realize, although the onset of the Great Depression put a severe crimp in the housing market, and many companies were unable to survive it. Some people now living in kit houses built at that time have determined the true origins of their home by discovering its design or a very similar one offered in a plan book of the period, several of which are reprinted and available today.

While the option of plan book kit homes became a popular way to obtain smaller dwellings such as bungalows, many larger two-story models were also marketed alongside them. Some of these larger homes were impressive, stylish residences, and nothing about this method of home construction negatively affected their quality. Even when compared to homes built from scratch with locally obtained materials, some would argue it was often better. Whether they were kit homes or not, the vast majority of new middle-class houses from bungalows to larger plans were outfitted with at least some prefabricated millwork elements for their interiors. These usually included doors and windows, plus specialty millwork items such as box beams, columns, corbels, brackets, fireplace mantels, bookcases, desks, and all sorts of other built-in cabinetry. First selected from catalogs, they were shipped in preassembled form by their manufacturers to building sites for installation. Although patronized directly by some homeowners who were involved in their own homes' construction, this industry's primary customers were the commercial builders who developed large housing tracts and generated steady repeat business.

Except for households with very generous budgets, it was uncommon to have most woodwork elements created locally or on-site by finish carpenters or cabinet-makers. Even at that time, the added labor costs for such custom work would have been well beyond the means of most households.

Bungaloid Homes: An Upward Expansion

Many real estate developers saw the promise of the bungalow's potential and quickly adopted its features, if not its plan, into their new homes. But they also realized that not everyone was going to be "bungalow material," and it was just a matter of how best to ensnare these other middle-class households that were still considered fair game for the new housing market. Many developers saw from the beginning that there was a market for so-called "bungaloid" houses. Outwardly, these had a close resemblance to their smaller relatives. Sharing similar features and detailing, these veered upward from the single-story format into a full two stories, usually with additional attic space. Bungaloid homes were geared toward not only those families who were interested in the latest housing trends and amenities, but also those who needed and could afford something a little larger.

Some early-twentieth-century households also tended to have more conservative tastes in their living arrangements. Since most middle-class people of that time would have grown up in a two-story home, there was already a sizeable market that opted for homes with a greater sense of division between various living spaces than could be found in a bungalow. One of the easiest and most proven ways to achieve this was with a traditional two-story floor plan. Another factor that favored the two-story house plan was that some households included some extended family members, in addition to a married couple and their children. Also, some middle-class homes might have employed a live-in servant as well, but these were dwindling in number by 1900. Households with these kinds of profiles were unlikely to fit into the average bungalow.

Bungaloid Home Planning

Generally, the homes built in the greatest numbers during the early twentieth century adopted the single-story bungalow-planning format, which usually had the smallest amount of square footage and used the least amount of building materials. The dimensions of a prospective building lot limited those of any bungalow plan. In some cases where bungalows were custom-designed for a larger site, their oft-touted economy of space and materials withered significantly if allowed to sprawl too far and wide in their plan. Furthermore, the most affordable lots in locations near the best job markets tended to be small and narrow, so most bungalows were destined to remain small homes on small lots. Usually the best bet for expanding one was to develop its attic into additional living space, usually bedrooms, and many original plans anticipated that option. Other bungalows were built with unusable crawl-space attics, and the cost of enlarging these was likely to be greater than moving up to a larger house anyway.

The most compact two-story house plans were designed to address the dilemma of a small lot's limitations. By including a second floor, the dimensions of the first-floor footprint of the home could be minimized, and more of the lot's open space could be preserved (SEE FIGURES 8 AND 9). As usually identified in their plan book, many home designs were specifically tailored to fit comfortably onto the most common standard lot sizes. For a minimal fee, purveyors of house plans offered to reverse the original layout into a mirror image, should that improve the orientation of the building design to the available lot.

On more spacious suburban or rural properties, house planning could be expanded up and out as far as the budget would allow (SEE FIGURES 15 AND 16). Some plan book designs were merely starting points for otherwise custom-built homes, for their pictures and floor plans were able to convey a sense of the homeowner's personal taste and planning expectations to their architect or builder, a process that would still work well for those interested in building a new home today. As many of the examples in this book illustrate so well, the influence of the Arts and Crafts movement was not limited by a home's scale or budget, but only by the imagination of those responsible for its creation.

A FAMILIAR FORM:
THE AMERICAN FOURSQUARE

ALONGSIDE THE BUNGALOW, the American foursquare claims its place as a classic housing type, and can be found in great abundance nearly everywhere. Most Americans would recognize these homes even if they don't know exactly what to call them. What defines a foursquare is its basic shape: a simple, square floor plan, with its overall width equal or close to its depth. When this formula varies, and it does, it is the home's depth that is extended, rather than its width. When it debuted in the early 1890s, many sported fancy late-Victorian-era details, but foursquares are most associated with the early twentieth century, and its simpler styles. During that time their construction peaked, and persisted up to about 1930.

Perhaps the most common exterior features of the foursquare are a wide front porch, a hipped (pyramidal) roof, and one or more dormers to light the attic level (SEE FIGURES 17 AND 20). Although some examples show the adaptability of the basic foursquare into much larger, and often more luxurious homes (SEE FIGURES 19 AND 22), most were designed and built to be solid, middle-class housing stock, and that is their primary claim to fame. Because of their no-nonsense form and expandable depth, many foursquares were enlisted as ideal, sturdy farmhouses, adding to their sensible workhorse cachet. The fact that such a regular, boxy form could be constructed almost as efficiently and economically as many single-story homes was not lost on real estate developers always looking for new ways to cut costs and sell more homes in the process.

Figure 17.

DRAWING OF A FOURSQUARE HOUSE
UNDER CONSTRUCTION (1926).

A Sears, Roebuck and Company plan book entitled Honor Built Modern Homes *included this illustration of a foursquare home, which could be procured by mail order as a complete Ready-cut package. The foursquare taking shape here has a characteristic full-width front porch, hipped roof, and attic-level dormer. The drawing was intended to demonstrate the efficiency of building houses with plans provided by Sears, who would ship standard-size, prenumbered, and precut lumber for a Ready-cut home's structural framing and provide other prefabricated house parts, such as doors, windows, and interior fittings directly to a building site for assembly, usually by local labor. By then, somewhat past its prime, the Craftsman style is implied in the tapering form of the porch column's supporting piers.*

Figure 18.

FOURSQUARE HOUSE IN PORTLAND, OREGON (CA. 1915).

Set on a lot of generous width, this example is a pleasing blend of various style influences. The roof's exposed rafter tails, the dormer's sloping-sided form, and the porch railing's plain spindles express the Craftsman taste. There is Colonial Revival influence reflected in the classical forms of the porch columns, and in the narrow-width clapboard siding seen above the porch roof. Extending around the house below the eaves, a wide band (or frieze) defined by a capped molding integrated into the second-floor window casings suggests a Prairie-style effect. Further articulated by its wider clapboard siding and darker paint color, its strong horizontality helps to lower the design. Centered within the porch, an angled bay window lends balance to the front, while other bays on the left side give it further interest.

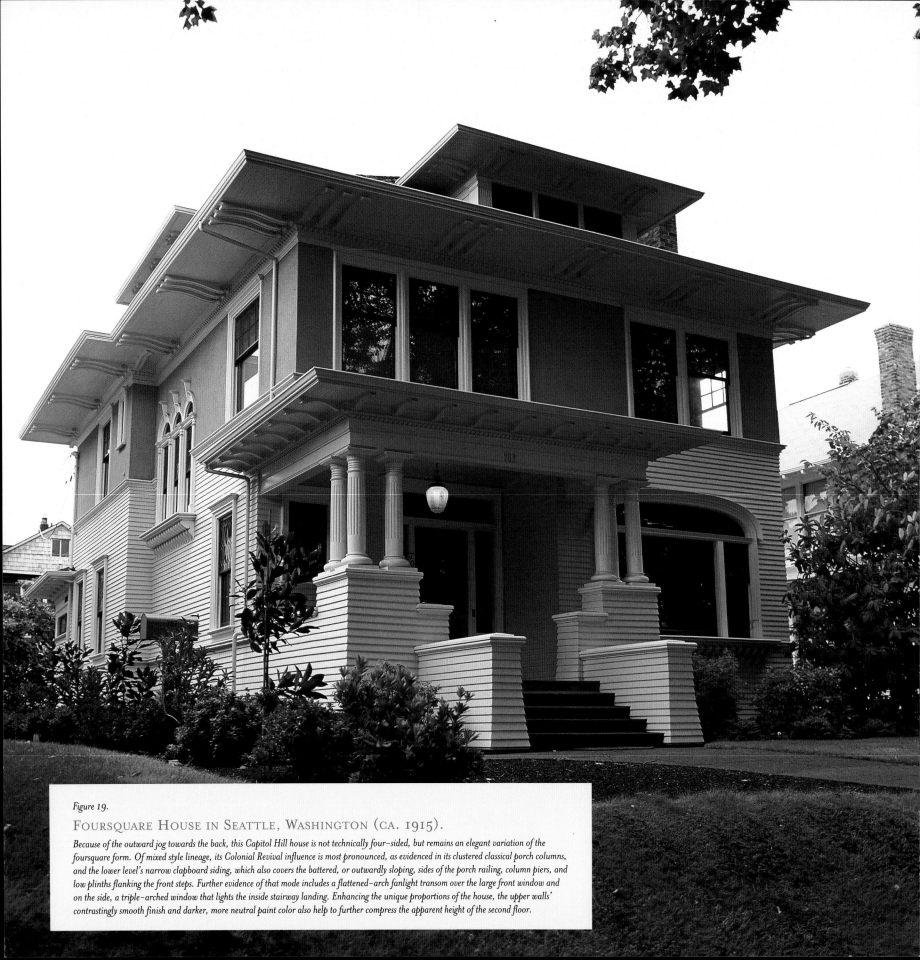

Figure 19.

FOURSQUARE HOUSE IN SEATTLE, WASHINGTON (CA. 1915).

Because of the outward jog towards the back, this Capitol Hill house is not technically four-sided, but remains an elegant variation of the foursquare form. Of mixed style lineage, its Colonial Revival influence is most pronounced, as evidenced in its clustered classical porch columns, and the lower level's narrow clapboard siding, which also covers the battered, or outwardly sloping, sides of the porch railing, column piers, and low plinths flanking the front steps. Further evidence of that mode includes a flattened-arch fanlight transom over the large front window and on the side, a triple-arched window that lights the inside stairway landing. Enhancing the unique proportions of the house, the upper walls' contrastingly smooth finish and darker, more neutral paint color also help to further compress the apparent height of the second floor.

Figure 20.

DESIGN FOR A FOURSQUARE HOUSE (1926).

One of the many plan book designs offered in Sears' Honor Built Modern Homes catalog, this one has a distinctly Craftsman-style treatment to its triple porch columns, which have outwardly flaring caps, and through-tenon detailing that links their midsections. A Ready-cut design, it was called "The Woodland" (or No. P3025), and priced at $2,491 as a complete package. Headlined as having "Nine Rooms and Bath," the house was listed as having wide steps to the front porch, divided upper lights on the window sash, and second-floor flower boxes among its "many attractive features." It was described as "being planned on strictly square lines" where "every foot of floor space is utilized to advantage, and the upkeep is small."

Functional Origins

Although the precise reason behind the foursquare's rather sudden appearance in the early 1890s remains debatable, it was most likely a logical result of ongoing advances in building technology and engineering rather than of any particular genius of architectural design. Originating in the Midwest, the mid-nineteenth century advent of "balloon-frame" construction (so named for the speed in which it allowed houses to go up) had greatly simplified wooden building techniques. A variation soon followed, called "western-platform framing" (most prevalent in southern and western regions), which enabled wooden buildings to be erected one floor at a time, with each floor a supporting platform for the one above it. The more recent development of nationwide standards for pre-milled lumber sizes, cut elsewhere and delivered ready for assembly at the building site, had helped stream-line construction, reduce waste, and further cut costs. With few, if any, jogs and angles in its pristinely regular form, the foursquare greatly assisted in its own building process with its predictable dimensions, and uncomplicated framing requirements (SEE FIGURE 17). For nearly four decades, the foursquare was a favorite mainstay moneymaker for homebuilders who, if asked about its source, could well have stated that it was simply "form follows function."

Like its exterior, the interior of a foursquare home tends to be formulaic—simple and functional. Perhaps the most typical plan has a room placed in each corner of the house (which allows for windows on two walls). As befits its numerical name, there are often (but not always) four rooms located on each of two floors. Generally reserved for storage, the third floor's attic space allows for the option of future expanded living space as needs grow. Usually placed to one side of the porch, the front door opens to an entry hall from which the stairway ascends along the outside wall. Opposite the stairway, a wide doorway opens directly into the living room (SEE FIGURE 21). From the front door, the kitchen is reached through a short hallway straight ahead, and occupies one of the rear corners of the house. The other rear corner contains the dining room, which is also open to the living room through a wide doorway. The stairway leads upstairs to a central hall connecting to

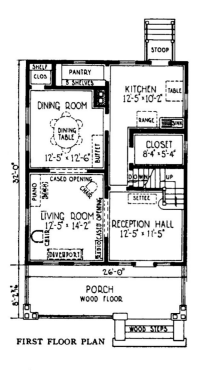

FIRST FLOOR PLAN

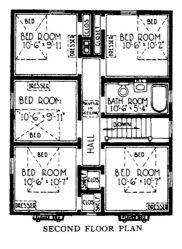

SECOND FLOOR PLAN

Figure 21.

FLOOR PLANS FOR THE FOURSQUARE HOUSE IN FIGURE 20.

This design packs a lot of practical utility into the arrangement of its two equally sized floors. Enhancing the feeling of space, wide-cased openings, trimmed out in wood without any doors, are used between the first floor's public rooms. There is an absence of built-in features such as colonnades, bookcases, or a dining room sideboard, which were falling out of favor by the 1920s. Upstairs, a central hallway leads to five very similarly sized bedrooms and a full bathroom. For a better idea of a house's actual scale, some plan books such as this one indicated with dotted lines possible placement of various typically sized, and most commonly found, furniture pieces on their floor plans.

FOURSQUARE: WHAT'S IN A NAME?

W hen they were originally built, a specific name eluded the American foursquare. Instead, they were simply referred to as a "square home," or as a home or plan "of the square type." With an endearingly folksy regionalism, some residents in various parts of the country invented their own nicknames for the familiar foursquares in their communities, such as the "Denver Box," Seattle's "Classic Box," and the "Cornbelt Cube" from Kansas and Iowa. In some places, these unofficial pet terms have continued to stubbornly resist any replacement. Finally in 1982, it was decisively dubbed the "American foursquare" in an article by Clem Labine and Patricia Poore, which appeared in the magazine *Old House Journal*. The magazine's editors at the time, Labine and Poore had cofounded the *Old House Journal* back in the 1970s as a resource for do-it-yourself homeowners of vintage American homes. Its mission was to educate, enlighten, and assist with advice and counsel on a wide variety of typical restoration and renovation issues and projects. The magazine's efforts have since inspired several other similar periodical ventures to share in its once-lonely mission. Long before the foursquare got its name, it was already on the radar screens of some old-house aspirants. Easily noticed because of its street presence, many were drawn to its straightforward simplicity. It seemed an answer to the needs of many looking for a roomy, older home with character and personality yet adaptable to the ways of modern living. With their plain, upright shape and simple roof configuration, foursquares tended to be less expensive to fix up and restore than earlier Victorian-era homes, most of which were far more complex in form and detailing. Certainly not the least of their appeal at that time was their affordability, for many foursquares were located in downtrodden, older urban neighborhoods.

By the time foursquares got their name,
the public's interest in America's vast stock
of vintage houses was already on the rise.

Figure 22. (opposite)

FOURSQUARE HOUSE IN DENVER, COLORADO (CA. 1915).

With its width and depth greater than that of the average foursquare, this house gains more horizontal proportions than most. Its design is a refined interpretation of the Craftsman style. The warm texture of the first floor's variegated red brick anchors the house, and to divide the materials, small wooden corbels underline the shingled second floor. Supported on trapezoidal piers of matching red brick, a finely detailed, full-width pergola (in lieu of a covered front porch) is employed. Of matching brick and sandstone, the low garden wall has been detailed to repeat the sloping piers of the pergola and to pull the architecture of the house out and into its lush landscape. Above the front door, a shallow arched overhang reflects some Colonial Revival influence.

the bedrooms, placed in each corner. Most foursquares were built with only one bathroom, usually placed between the stairway and one of the bedrooms. Opening off the upstairs hall, the attic stairway was usually concealed by a closable door. By today's standards, bedroom closet space tends to be minimal but adequate.

Most variations of the foursquare's basic arrangement occur when the stairway is placed in a less prominent location. In lieu of an entry hall, some foursquare entries are directly into their living rooms, which then also function as the primary circulation space to other rooms. In such plans, the living room usually extends across the full width of the house, but remains open to the dining room towards one end. A wide doorway between these two rooms amplifies the effect of the actual space, and creates an open sequence of primary living spaces that recalls bungalow floor plans (SEE FIGURES 24–26). Foursquare plans without separate entry halls may place the stairway in open view of the living room, or less conspicuously, off a hallway adjacent to the kitchen. In the manner of many Colonial Revival floor plans, a center hall plan requires an extra width that only larger foursquare variations allow. This more traditional arrangement places the entry hall at the center of the house, the stairway along one of the entry's side walls, and the living and dining rooms set on either side.

The Bungalow's Big Brother

To help place the American foursquare into this book's context, it is helpful to think of it as a slightly older sibling of the bungalow. Although they have quite different outward appearances, they share numerous parallels. For example, the popularity of each house type straddled the turn of the last century, with some examples of each built before 1900 and the majority after that date. When both were darlings of the new-house market, they shared similar reputations as good value for the money spent. Designs for each house type were marketed heavily in countless plan books, and each was among the most popular of the all-prefabricated kit-home designs in their heyday between 1900 and 1930 (SEE FIGURES 17, 20 AND 21). Foursquares and bungalows can often boast of similar interior features such as built-ins, and both were lauded for the space-saving practicality of their floor plans. Both also achieved great popularity across the country, and were built in tremendous numbers. While a few regional characteristics and differences do occur, bungalows and foursquares each display a remarkably consistent sense of scale and recognizable streetside demeanor.

Many inner-city foursquares were originally designed and built as a two-family duplex, with a floor-through apartment (or flat) on each level. This dual-unit identity wasn't always immediately apparent, for many of them shared a single front door. This ensured the building an outward appearance of a more desirable single-family home, and allowed such a duplex to blend easily into a neighborhood of mostly single-family homes. While planning variations do exist, the shared front door of most duplex foursquares opens to a common entry hall, from which one door leads directly into the lower unit, and another to the staircase of the upper one. While most foursquares were built with a wide first-floor front porch, some have a full-width porch on each floor, which tends to make the dual-family status of these homes more outwardly apparent.

By the time foursquares got their name, the public's interest in America's vast stock of vintage houses was already on the rise. Stirred by growing nationwide reassess-ments of decaying, older, inner-city neighborhoods, many began to see that these areas could again be the vital, respectable areas they had once been. The prospect of so-called gentrification of many inner-city neighborhoods proved a pivotal moment for America's historic preservation movement, enabling their noble mission to be expanded into a whole new rank of middle-class population, who could have ended up as apathetic residents of suburbia, but chose the city instead. Initially, the public's interest was focused on homes of the Victorian era, whose quaint character and various styles dominated many older neighborhoods. Foursquares were there too, but many were built later as infill among earlier homes, or as part of other early-twentieth-century developments adjacent to Victorian areas. Many of these had been subjected to the same neglect and abuse as their Victorian neighbors, commonly fated to be chopped into small apartments, or operated as dismal rooming houses.

At a time when so many urban neighborhoods were on the brink of despair, a new group of old-house fans materialized, and almost singlehandedly helped turn the tide in favor of saving and improving old houses and old neighborhoods that had nearly been given up as lost. Sometimes described as urban pioneers, these adventuresome souls, beginning in the 1960s, had already begun to see the potential and eventual financial upside of moving into such areas. Consistent across the country, the demographics of this group were dominated by the younger generation (notably, this group included a significant number of gay people among its mix of stalwart singles and couples). The homes they were drawn to were usually much larger and more architecturally interesting than what most could afford in the better neighborhoods. After making the leap to purchase an old, crumbling home for a bargain price, the task of restoring and renovating got underway. Often by necessity, it was through using their own hands and logging in hours of sweat equity that many were able to transform formerly lifeless shells, many of them American foursquares, into stylish urban habitats brimming with historic character.

Figure 23.

THE ARTHUR B. BENTON HOUSE, LOS ANGELES, CALIFORNIA (1896, WITH 1912 ADDITIONS).

Designed by noted Southern California architect, Arthur Burnett Benton (1857–1927), this house is a variation of a foursquare. First designed for a client, the house was later acquired by Benton, who remodeled and enlarged it as his own residence and studio. Unified by its shingled skin, the design features a hipped roof, enlivened by a subtle upward kick to its outer edges, which is also applied to a tiny, tower-like dormer. Helping to exaggerate this effect are the sharply pointed metal finials on the roof's peaks. Exposed rafter tails are in the Craftsman manner, as is the emphatic row of struc-tural beams with shaped ends that project beyond the offset porch's shallow recess; a solid covering makes a porch awning. Benton is best known as the architect of the Mission Inn at Riverside, California (1902 and later), a celebrated example of the Mission Revival style applied to a grand public building.

Figure 24.

FOURSQUARE HOUSE IN
MINNEAPOLIS, MINNESOTA (1918).

Sited in the city's Bryn Mawr district, this house was built by May E. Benedict, and it shows that not all foursquares have the typical hipped-roof configuration. Instead, because of its side-facing gabled roof with a deep overhang and front dormer, this house has some of the ground-hugging character of Craftsman bungalows, albeit enhanced by the uphill perspective of this view. Composed with complete symmetry, the façade's boldly geometric character is expressed in the massively scaled detailing of its full-width front porch. Centered on the house, the front steps bisect the sloping portion of the front yard, which was recently studded with rocks and boulders and replanted as a shade-loving garden. A low hedge acts as a privacy buffer at the top of the steps, screening a level lawn area.

Figure 25. (opposite)

LIVING ROOM AND DINING ROOM OF THE FOURSQUARE HOUSE
IN FIGURE 24.

As with many foursquare plans, the living room extends across the full width of the house. A fully developed expression of
the Craftsman style, this interior's scale, detailing, and open planning recalls that of many bungalows. Viewed from the
front door at its center, this end of the room is oriented around a simple brick-faced fireplace set between built-in bookcases of matching height, all unified beneath a room-wide mantel that extends under the small side windows. Contributing
to the inviting atmosphere are warmly vivid paint colors that flatter the darker woodwork. They are only a small part
of the major transformation made to this house by its current owners, who have fully restored its luster throughout after
acquiring it in 1997.

Figure 26.

LIVING ROOM AND STAIRWAY OF THE FOURSQUARE HOUSE
IN FIGURE 24.

From a similar spot by the front door, this view shows the Craftsman-style features of the living room's other
half. At right, a piano window shows the reason for its name. The lower staircase structure, opposite the
front door, incorporates a built-in bench (housing vents instead of storage space), a closet with an original
beveled mirror-inset door, and a square-spindled screen wall, (a stylish Craftsman-style device that shields
the stairs as they rise to the second floor). The lower landing, up a couple of steps from the living room, also
connects to the kitchen through the doorway, back down another couple of steps. Other than through the
living room, the dining room may also be reached through another door from the kitchen. A rear sunroom,
added in 1926, also connects to the dining room and a pergola-covered garden patio.

NATURE COMES HOME:
RUSTIC STYLE INFLUENCE

DESPITE THE RUSTIC STYLE'S TYPICAL USE of natural building materials and exposed structural elements, its sources have no direct connection to the Arts and Crafts movement. In fact, the origin of Rustic design and detailing predates that later movement. However, the Rustic style does have good reason to be included in this book's Arts and Crafts discussion, for it was applied to some early-twentieth-century buildings that also evoke an Arts and Crafts sensibility.

Because the two terms are closely related, it is important to note that certain homes may be alternately described as either Rustic or Adirondack style. The more general term of the two, *Rustic* may be used to describe a wider variety of structures and their interiors, hence, its use in the title of this chapter. The term Adirondack style, taking its name from the range of mountains in upstate New York, was coined to describe a specific style of regional vernacular architecture, interiors and furniture that utilized logs and tree branches, usually left in their natural state, in both structural and decorative ways.

The Adirondack style became a popular choice for that mountainous region's resort hotels, for sprawling family compounds called camps, and also for smaller-scale summer cabins beginning in the late nineteenth century. Between 1870 and 1930, the

Figure 27.

THE LOG HOUSE AT CRAFTSMAN FARMS,
PARSIPPANY, NEW JERSEY (1911).

Gustav Stickley's own home was highlighted in the November issue of Craftsman *magazine. Constructed of chestnut logs felled on the property, the house also features locally gathered fieldstone on the building foundation and chimneys. The exposed-log first floor comprises a long, covered porch, now glass-enclosed (on the far left), and a large living room at the center, anchored by two massive stone fireplaces with copper hoods. The dining room is the same length, but narrower, and the stone-walled, oversized kitchen is in back. An open stairway in the living room leads to the second-floor bedrooms (there are no service stairs). The Log House at Craftsman Farms is home to the Stickley Museum and is open to the public (see "Stickley's Log Legacy" on page 39).*

Figure 28.

RIORDAN MANSION, FLAGSTAFF, ARIZONA (1904).

This exceptional Arts and Crafts home was built as a double house for brothers Timothy and Michael Riordan, early settlers and prominent businessmen. The use of natural logs reflects their success in the logging business, although there is also extensive use of stone, cut lumber, and wood shingles. Since the brothers married sisters Caroline and Elizabeth Metz, they decided to build two interconnected, but self sufficient, homes, large enough for both of their households, including servants. Charles Whittlesey (1867–1941), the architect of the Grand Canyon's famous 1905 El Tovar Hotel, was their designer. The Riordans' home, named Kinlichi, comprises 13,000 square feet and almost forty rooms. The original Arts and Crafts furnishings and finishes are remarkably intact. The Riordan Mansion is open to the public as a house museum.

Figure 29.

HOUSE IN PASADENA, CALIFORNIA (1909).

Constructed by the Milwaukee Building Company, this house is a good example of a Craftsman-style crossover, detailed in the Rustic style. The Rustic elements subtly blend into the lines of the shingled, gabled structure, which otherwise resembles many larger Arts and Crafts homes. Natural logs of varying diameters and lengths are extensively used; some are split lengthwise and serve as door and window trim. Large logs placed as columns flank the recessed front door (obscured, at center). These support a horizontal log that extends across the front of the house, terminating at the outside corner (at right) atop another vertical log support. Among other log details are the large angled brackets (braces) supporting the deep roof eaves. At the upper-right corner, a sleeping porch/playroom supplements four second-floor bedrooms.

Figure 30.

CHIEF HOSA LODGE, GOLDEN, COLORADO (1918).

On the National Register of Historic Places, this Rustic-style structure was commissioned by the city of Denver for visitors to its mountain park system that was established in 1916. The building is named to honor a local Arapahoe Chief named Little Raven, who signed an 1871 peace treaty with President U. S. Grant. Hosa means "One Who Fights for Peace, Honor, Dignity, Principle." The lodge's style was intended to mix Native American and European cultures, and was the first public building designed by French architect Jacques Benedict. Constructed of hand-quarried local stone, the first floor features tapering buttresses at its outside corners. Local trees provided the natural log details. Two clipped (jerkin-headed) gables, traditional to Europe, are on the front façade (which extends to the left), and an open terrace with spectacular mountain views fronts the building.

Adirondacks were at their peak as a fashionable retreat for some of America's wealthiest families, such as the Huntingtons, Whitneys, Carnegies, and Vanderbilts. Owners and guests could rough it while being coddled by large staffs of domestic servants. Especially fine camps were built for J. P. Morgan and Marjorie Merriweather Post. A primary force in the early development of the Adirondacks, Thomas C. Durant was a railroad builder who helped transform that remote wilderness into an easily accessible playground. William West Durant, his son and collaborator, built some of the most notable camps, including Sagamore Hill, which, when under financial duress, he sold to Alfred G. Vanderbilt in 1901.

In their overall form, some of these homes show an influence of the Swiss Chalet, as does Sagamore Hill. More common are structures with quirkier proportions, and whimsically inventive Rustic detailing that recall folk art. Similar aesthetics guided the design of many original period furnishings, which are now rare and highly collectible. Their tradition lives on in similarly inspired new work by contemporary craftspeople. While many significant examples of Adirondack-style homes in and around that region have survived, battles to protect them from harm or disappearance are still being fought. Well documented in various books, the architecture and furniture of the Adirondacks is a fascinating topic on its own, but except as an influence, is not a primary focus in this book.

Since its original examples were created, the Adirondack style's picturesque look has traveled to many other regions of the country, and is still especially popular for vacation homes with mountainous or lakeside settings. Although quite different in its character, another familiar use of the term applies to the Adirondack chair— a form of outdoor seating that uses wide boards for its arms, its jauntily angled and slightly fan-shaped back, and its seat. Matching footstools and sometimes two-seater versions are often added to make a set. Despite their relatively simple form and great popularity since the early twentieth century, Adirondack chairs cannot claim a specifically Arts and Crafts provenance.

Figure 31.

INTERIOR DETAIL OF THE CHIEF HOSA LODGE.

Most of the original lodge interior is characterized by exposed rustic-wood ceiling structures with natural log trusses. Pictured is one of the two gabled areas that comprise each end of the building (Figure 29 shows the outside view). The room also has a large stone fireplace. Between the two gabled ends, the main entrance opens into a generous central rectangular room, which is also its primary assembly space. Later additions have been made to the back of the lodge. First a museum, the lodge has been alternately used as a restaurant, chapel, bordello, and gambling hall. Currently, it is operated as a venue for private gatherings and special events, and also adjoins a campground.

SOURCES OF THE RUSTIC STYLE

W hile its most distant origins are far from certain, a similar application of building materials now associated with the Rustic style put in brief appearances in a few fanciful eighteenth-century European paintings and book illustrations. Although some of these structures may have only been imagined, the originals have long since vanished. Their construction employed unfinished, rough-looking logs to construct small, open-air garden structures, which in England were called *follies*, and their function was comparable to that of a gazebo.

Departing from the French-derived geometric formality that preceded it, a vogue developed for asymmetrical, natural-looking landscapes such as those designed by Capability Brown for large country estates in eighteenth-century England. This style favored the use of a folly to help terminate a vista, or perhaps gesture towards an appealing distant destination. Essentially, these were visual punctuation marks in larger landscape schemes, but they were also good opportunities to experiment on a playful level with real architecture. A good example of one such folly would be made of rough-hewn logs assembled into a witty parody of a tiny classical temple, a tongue-in-cheek reference to the theory that ancient Greek temples may have evolved from primitive wooden structures, in which tall tree trunks were the early forerunners of classical columns, an intriguing theory that remains speculative.

By the early nineteenth century, some evidence of the Rustic style began to appear around smaller-scale American country houses and cottages, and was most likely to show up in garden locations. Used for decorative effect, it was applied to designs for arbors, trellises, fences, and gates. The Rustic sensibility in America emerged as a way of giving some tangible form to a trend towards Romanticism that persisted into the early Victorian era. Mostly a reaction to the rapidly emerging industrialization that seemed to be changing everything familiar, the manifestations of the Romantic movement were tinged with notions of fantasy and escape, often into an imagined past. Affecting public taste in all the arts, it particularly celebrated and idealized the beauty of nature, and especially wilderness, as an omnipotent force that dwells among us. While never a full-blown architectural style of housing at that time, the early influences of a Rustic sensibility were most fashionable as adjuncts to natural garden settings. In what today seems a humorously ironic violation of every tenet of the Arts and Crafts movement, some Rustic Victorian—era garden furniture was constructed of purposely irregular tree branches, rendered quite realistically in cast iron.

Rustic Style Goes National

By the early twentieth century, the proven appeal of the Rustic-design sensibility as applied to "architecture of leisure" did not go unnoticed by the United States government, which chose to build lodges and other visitor service buildings in the Rustic style, often of log construction, in America's growing collection of national parks. Numbers of automobile-borne tourists were rapidly growing, and the parks were a resounding success with the middle-class public seeking affordable vacation spots. Designated in 1872 as the world's first national park, Yellowstone National Park in Wyoming became a model for many other parks that followed. The Old Faithful Inn (1903–1904) at Yellowstone was designed by architect Robert Reamer, and is one of the most ambitious and successful examples of its kind. The inn remains a celebrated expression of the so-called "National Park" style, also nicknamed "parkitecture," for its consistent popularity at such sites.

Today, the terms *Rustic* and *Adirondack* are used, sometimes interchangeably, to describe the style of buildings that are of log construction for at least part of their structure. In several examples, smaller-diameter tree trunks are incorporated into some of the design elements, such as for brackets, or framed door and window openings (SEE FIGURE 29). In more overtly picturesque examples, irregular tree branches may serve as lightweight adjuncts to large-sized structural elements, or perhaps as additional flourishes of decorative detail on interiors and exteriors. Other applications seen in lodge-like interiors showcase natural logs as structural materials, and present them with a minimum of fussiness (SEE FIGURE 31).

Figure 32.

HIWAN HOMESTEAD, EVERGREEN, COLORADO (CA. 1890S–1918).

Built entirely of logs from trees harvested on the property, this rambling Rustic style structure is only partially visible in this view. Mary Neosho Williams, a Civil War widow, and her daughter, Josepha, a medical doctor nicknamed Dr. Jo, bought the original one-room cabin as a summer home. In the 1890s, Scottish carpenter Jock Spence enlarged the structure. When Mrs. Williams entertained, her visiting relatives and friends were housed in tents in a nearby grove of trees. In 1896, Dr. Jo married Charles Winfred Douglas, an Episcopal minister. The couple had Jock Spence further enlarge the place after Mrs. Williams died in 1914. A chapel built in 1918 in the north octagonal tower (one of two) completed the additions. Dr. Jo died in 1928, and the place was sold to the Darst Buchanans of Oklahoma. Mrs. Buchanan named the property Hiwan Ranch (an old Anglo-Saxon term), and it became a working farm, home to prize Hereford cattle. The Buchanan family sold the property in 1974, and the following year it was opened to the public as a house museum.

The Log Cabin Connection

Concerning its impact on later domestic architecture, a far more enduring and endearing aspect of the Rustic style is its association with that particularly American icon, the log cabin. Perhaps most famously known as the type of rural house where Abraham Lincoln was born, these rough-and-tumble structures are now beloved symbols of our country and strongly associated with the lure of the wild American frontier. Although log cabins are highly romanticized today, most examples were practical, durable solutions to serious housing challenges facing early settlers. Emblematic of living off the land where such timber was plentiful, log cabins were admirable models of economy. Among the smallest in scale are the earliest examples, which were also the most primitive in their amenities, for many were built with dirt floors, no windows, or a lack of other basic features.

Logs are used to create the walls of the house by stacking rows of horizontally placed, similarly-sized logs up to the level of the roof (SEE FIGURE 32). Each layer of logs is secured at the corners by a system of interlocking notches, creating a remarkably strong building not likely to get blown down in any storm. After the gaps and chinks between the logs were filled in, usually with a mixture of clay and straw called "daub," log homes had surprisingly good insulating properties that were effective in the harsh climates of the forested areas where they were most likely to be built (SEE FIGURE 32–33). If workable material was locally abundant, stone foundations were sometimes built for otherwise log-constructed homes. Especially evocative components of the Rustic-style vocabulary are sturdy combinations of wood and stone (SEE FIGURES 28 AND 30).

Although similar examples of log construction had evolved over time as vernacular wooden housing in other parts of the world, such as Scandinavia, the imagery of a log cabin evoked strong nationalistic feelings among Americans by the early twentieth century. At that time, because of the Rustic style's association with natural materials and exposed joinery, it made a perfectly logical, eminently compatible influence to that of the Arts and Crafts movement, even if these two hadn't

Figure 34. (opposite)

DINING ROOM OF THE HIWAN HOMESTEAD.

Placed at the inside corner of the roughly L-shaped building, the dining room was among the post-1914 additions and directly adjoins the living room. Retreating from the Rustic style, the room shows a Craftsman influence. The angled form of the ceiling reflects its structure, but here more refined finish carpentry conceals it. A stepped design on the wooden ceiling medallion, repeated elsewhere inside and out, adapts a Native American motif and complements the artifacts. Above built-in window seats, diamond-paned casement windows line the room's left side and wrap around the corner. The pair of wood fins at left, with stepped tops and painted decoration, allowed the window between to be slightly indented to avoid a tree, which still survives. In the far right corner is a now-blocked door to a serving pantry, and access to the rest of the house is through a door to the right.

Figure 33.

LIVING ROOM OF THE HIWAN HOMESTEAD.

Tours of the Hiwan Homestead Museum begin in this room, which is part of the first 1890s addition. It was used as a multi-purpose space until the later additions were made. The original log cabin is located behind the stone fireplace. Although partially covered, some structural elements are visible in the open-peaked ceiling. The wall at right indicates its log construction, and the rough fieldstone fireplace also evokes the Rustic style. At the side of a shed-roof dormer, the odd triangular window at right was an ingenious way to bring more light into a fairly dark room. The small staircase accesses a former bedroom, which is inaccessible from other added-on second-floor rooms. Along with Craftsman-style pieces, artwork, and personal possessions, portions of the former owners' extensive collection of Native American pottery, textiles, and other artifacts are displayed around the room.

been originally connected. When these influences were combined, it was often for the country or vacation homes of well-to-do families (SEE FIGURE 32). Considered by tastemakers of the day as appropriate furnishings in the Arts and Crafts spirit, if not a true part of it, collecting Native American artifacts such as handcrafted baskets, pottery, blankets, and rugs became a fashionable pursuit. Especially compatible in Rustic-style settings, many great collections of rare or priceless artifacts were formed during the period. One side effect of these artifacts' collectibility was that it encouraged a continuation of old craft traditions among many Native Americans, whose authentic but newly made souvenirs were sold to tourists (SEE FIGURES 33–35).

Stickley's Log Legacy

One of the best and most significant examples of a house that deftly merges elements of the Rustic style with an Arts and Crafts sensibility is the Log House at Craftsman Farms. Featured in a 1911 issue of the *Craftsman* magazine (SEE FIGURE 27), this house had then just been completed by Gustav Stickley on a rural tract of land in an area that is now part of Parsippany-Troy Hills, New Jersey. Located a reasonable distance from his business concerns in New York City, Stickley purchased the 650-acre parcel in 1907, and first imagined it as the site of a rural community of craftspeople, made self-sufficient by their various craft skills and output, growing their own food, and raising their own livestock. This idea evolved into another in which Craftsman Farms would become a kind of vocational school where masters of craft in various skills would train local young men. While also learning marketable agricultural skills, they would help staff and run the farm in the process.

While neither of these ideas ever materialized, Stickley did see his property become a working farm, and he decided to move his family into the log house at Craftsman Farms instead. However, their stay there was destined to be brief; it lasted only about five years. As a result of his bankruptcy, Stickley was forced to sell the entire property. Despite the extent of his fame and influence up to that time, he was fated to live out his days in Syracuse, New York, in relative obscurity, quite disconnected from the market forces that had once made him so successful.

Figure 35. (opposite)

BEDROOM FIREPLACE IN THE HIWAN HOMESTEAD.

Part of the later additions, this second-floor bedroom has exposed structure but utilizes smooth, machine-cut lumber. The room's fireplace would be quite plain without the diverse collection of Native American—made tiles pressed into its concrete face. Created for the tourist market to support the tribes, such items were adapted from traditional crafts and were avidly collected by Arts and Crafts devotees. Fashioned into a portière (doorway drapery), a blanket screens a corner closet.

Figure 36.

CHAPEL IN THE HIWAN HOMESTEAD.

This Gothic-inspired room on the north octagonal tower's second floor is the most dramatic and finely crafted in the house. Extensively used, the chapel was convenient in a remote area that had few churches. Paneled entirely in wood, the room's structural elements are expressed in a series of soaring beams and braces that curve upward in graceful, two-story arcs. The provided seating is expectedly austere. Gothic-style stone tracery inspired the pairs of leaded-glass windows (also visible in Figure 32). Half-round dormer windows near the ceiling provide additional light. Suspended fabric banners with colorful appliquéd designs recall medieval heraldic motifs. An altar alcove is out of view to the left. Next to the organ is a door to a staircase leading to a study below, where Canon Douglas prepared his sermons.

CRAFTSMAN STYLE:
CLASSIC ARTS AND CRAFTS HOMES

AS IT DID FOR SO MANY BUNGALOWS, the Craftsman style brought the greatest measure of Arts and Crafts influence to many larger homes of the same period. Starting out as the brand name of Gustav Stickley's business in 1900, the term *Craftsman* stayed at the center of everything else he went on to do; he assigned the name to all things he designed and marketed, from furniture to house plans. Buoyed by the turn of the new century, he fervently believed the time was right to deliver his personal vision of an ideal modern lifestyle to as many Americans as possible. Inspired as he was, Stickley also proved to be a shrewd businessman. While it lasted, his undeniable zeal for his mission had a lot to do with his success. By preaching tirelessly to the loyal readers of his nationally distributed magazine, *The Craftsman,* about the advantages of living a life infused with "all things Craftsman," Stickley believed in his concepts and designs, and felt they could never go out of style. In the short term, he was proven quite wrong, but from today's perspective there is much evidence to support that he was right.

A Typical Home among the Flowers, California.

Figure 37.

POSTCARD VIEW OF "A TYPICAL HOME AMONG THE FLOWERS, CALIFORNIA" (CA. 1910).

Amidst a parklike setting, this imposing two-story Craftsman-style house looms on the horizon. With the exception of the larger Greene and Greene–designed homes, grand impressions like this were not typical of most Craftsman-style postcard examples. Characteristic features of this style include multiple gables (with a shallow pitch typical of California), deep overhanging eaves, exposed rafter tails, and window casings with their lintels (tops) extended to either side. The roof awning over the front entry appears to be cantilevered off the face of the building and supported by chains, a design detail seen in some houses by Pasadena architect Alfred Heineman (SEE FIGURE 67). This building's color scheme looks paler than might be expected, possibly because artists often invented the coloration for vintage postcards rather than depict reality. Such imagery promoted California while spreading awareness of its latest housing trends.

Figure 38.

HOUSE IN PORTLAND, OREGON (CA. 1915).

With abundant Craftsman-style details, this house in the Mount Baker area is sited uphill, making its features easy to spot. For horizontal emphasis, the walls have shingle courses of alternating widths. Simple shed-style forms are employed for the front-porch and side bay window roofs. The shaped ends of the exposed rafter tails suggest clothespins. The fascia boards (bargeboards) of the front gable and side dormer are dotted with keyed tenon details, more typical of Arts and Crafts furniture. Oversized, angled brackets extend outward from the walls to support the fascia boards, and their basic design is also repeated on the brackets under the side bay window. The scale and detailing of the porch's posts and railing is robust yet simple. The upper front gable's diamond-paned attic windows suggests an English or Colonial Revival influence.

From Brand Name to Household Word

Even before his business had fallen from its height by 1916, the world at large had already snatched the term *craftsman* away from Stickley's exclusive grasp, perhaps because his marketing powers had been a bit too persuasive and pervasive for his own good. At that time, he was unable to prevent or curtail others from co-opting the efforts of his vision for their own gain, and many of his furniture designs and house plans were flagrantly copied. In the transition of the word *craftsman* from a brand name to a generic household word, it lost something of the power and focus it held under the watchful eye of its creator. But the popularity of his Craftsman-style homes and others inspired by them didn't die along with Stickley's business. While the style had already peaked in popularity by the time of World War I, it continued to be considered one of America's mainstream housing styles into the 1920s. However, the reputation and public perception that Craftsman homes had enjoyed as progressive modern dwellings during most of Stickley's stewardship of their creation had already shifted by then. The Craftsman style had ruled its roost in the housing coop for nearly two decades, and changing public taste indicated a desire to move on.

The 1920s were a vibrant period that in many ways reinvented American life forever. That decade also witnessed the last gasps of Arts and Crafts influence before the Great Depression set in. Still shaken by the disasters of World War I, the country had survived and seemed intent on getting on with life and industry. Automobiles were now a common middle-class amenity, and new kinds of influential cultural infusions were afoot; radio programming was replacing other forms of entertainment in American homes, and the burgeoning movie industry eagerly delivered all the escapist fantasy the public now craved.

In this climate, the Craftsman style was increasingly perceived as dated and out of step with the times. Fueled by public demand for greater and different choices, popular housing styles took a turn toward several influences of historic revivalism. This was a real setback for long-time followers of the Craftsman style, and many would have to wait for the coming Modern movement to feel progressive once again. Because they had grown up with it, the younger generation of prospective new homeowners had a very different impression. Instead they were drawn to different styles, especially those derived from a more distant past, which many found stylish in their reinvention, and at the same time comfortingly familiar.

The Craftsman Style: A Visual Vocabulary

What are some of the defining characteristics of the Craftsman style? What comes to mind first is its general air of modesty and restraint, whether applied to a bungalow or to the following examples of larger homes. Never intended to be a showy style, it quietly interpreted the aesthetic tenets of the Arts and Crafts movement, using simple, natural materials, and straightforward massing in a home's overall composition. Many consider this style to be quite plain (if not severe), but when its language is understood, then simplicity can be one of its greatest charms. Despite popular modern associations with homey comforts and coziness, Craftsman-style homes were considered among the most modern of their day. Another quality also found in bungalows is a sense of connection to the surrounding garden and landscape, whether communicated through materials, adjoining outdoor living spaces (such as porches and terraces), multiple outside doors, or a combination of all of these. A common observation of many Craftsman homes of any scale is how they seem to nestle into their settings as comfortably as if they had grown from the earth.

Not always easy to define because of their great diversity, the so-called purest examples of this style are conspicuously absent of design elements borrowed from an earlier historic style. However, houses that don't fit this criteria should not be considered in a lesser light; there were many larger homes designed with quite a different take on an Arts and Crafts sensibility other than entirely Craftsman. Many of these are intriguingly effective combinations of Craftsman-style elements used along with others that are obviously borrowed from an earlier historic style. For example, some homes were designed as interpretations of a historically inspired style on their exteriors, but their interiors are predominantly expressive of the Craftsman style. Still considered to be Arts and Crafts homes, such crossover examples as these (arranged according to their major style influence) are the focus of the discussions and photos of the chapters that follow.

As with bungalows, among the most characteristic architectural forms of larger Craftsman-style homes is some form of a gabled roof. Interpreted in many ways, their roofs can be configured with forward-facing or side-facing gables, L-shaped with three or more gables, U-shaped with perhaps four gables, with smaller double or triple dormer-like gables across the front (SEE FIGURE 62) or with crossing gables facing in four opposite directions (SEE FIGURES 39 AND 67). Some Craftsman

Figure 39.

HOUSE IN PORTLAND, OREGON (1910).

Located in the Irvington district, this Craftsman-style home was designed by Raymond Hockenberry. August Olson, a logging executive, commissioned the home and it is sited on a raised corner lot. The crossing-gabled form of its roof and exposed structure of the deep eaves are well displayed, while the absence of fascia boards gives the roof a thinner, lighter quality. Its pitch is repeated on the front porch roof, which has an exposed structural truss in its gable. The combination of highly textured clinker brick and stone used on the porch columns and chimney contributes an expressively organic character to the house. The smooth, light-colored first floor stucco contrasts with the deep brick red on the foundation level clapboard siding and the shingled walls of the upper story.

homes have even more complex rooflines. To help break up their larger-scaled mass, some use multiple gables, sometimes set at different levels, including that of the porch (SEE FIGURE 8). Others were designed to incorporate a combination of hipped and gabled roof forms. The clipped (jerkin-headed) gable, a traditional roof detail borrowed from English and other European sources, was used to help reduce the visual weight of the roof, and to lower the effect of its height (SEE FIGURE 7). The pitch of Craftsman-style roofs also varies. In warmer climates, it tends to be set at a shallower angle, which helps reinforce a feeling of horizontality and also reduces the sightlines of the roofing material, which isn't usually a focal point (SEE FIGURES 37, 41, 66 AND 67). In colder regions, steeper roof pitches were favored to allow excessive build-up of snow to be more easily shed.

In addition to their gable configurations, many Craftsman homes feature dormers sprouting from their roofs, which suggests there may be additional living space contained within the attic level (SEE FIGURES 2 AND 43). The shapes of dormers can vary considerably; many tend to be hipped or gabled, but the one most associated with the Craftsman style is the simple shed-roof dormer (SEE FIGURES 5 AND 27). Its advantage over most other dormer shapes is that its roof pitch can be more easily adjusted and its width extended to help further open up and light the upper-floor rooms. Usually shed roof dormers are the least obtrusive variety to add on to an existing building. Shed roofs frequently appear on projecting bay windows and sometimes on front porches (SEE FIGURES 10, 38 AND 46).

As with the bungalow, front porches are a ubiquitous feature of many larger Craftsman homes, and serve much of the same purpose in terms of their use. However, the porches of larger homes are frequently design devices to help minimize the homes' apparent size (SEE FIGURE 8). While many porches extend across the entire front of the house, as with most bungalows and many foursquares, some are used in various other configurations to further manipulate the proportions of the façade to better advantage (SEE FIGURE 39). Occasionally, façades are defined by porches that are stacked one on another, allowing a more private outdoor space accessible from the second floor (SEE FIGURE 42).

In some examples, front porches are built with open-beamed pergola-type roofs, from partial to full-width, allowing more natural light to be admitted into the interior (SEE FIGURE 22). Some porch roofs extend beyond one side of the house, creating a *porte-cochère* (covered side driveway). This feature is practical for dropping off passengers, or hauling groceries out of the rain before proceeding to stow the car in a rear garage. On some bungalows, *porte-cochères* were used for the same reason, as well as to help give them more horizontal emphasis. On larger homes, they tend to make a grander impression, exaggerating both the home's width and its overall sense of scale (SEE FIGURES 122 AND 148).

Porches need columns for support, and these provide the same opportunity to make a design statement on larger Craftsman homes as they do on bungalows. The most definitive Craftsman-style column shape is square and often tapering. If the house is faced in brick, then matching material is usually repeated on the porch columns. The irregular, jagged textures and deep variegated colors of so-called

Figure 40.

LIVING ROOM OF THE PORTLAND HOUSE IN FIGURE 39.

From the wide center hall, open to views of adjacent rooms, this home exudes a feeling of spaciousness. As one faces the living room, the dining room is directly behind, and an open stairway and door to the kitchen are on the right. The living room is dramatically framed by a broad doorway, fitted with a colonnade of square, tapering columns. The living room fireplace, in axial alignment with the doorway and lit by period sconces, makes a bold statement with its original, full-height ceramic-tile facing. Glazed in matte-finish, mottled shades of blue and green, its Arts and Crafts character is enriched by the riveted brass trim strips that outline its edges, including those of the fireplace opening, and the mantel's display niche.

clinker brick (once considered discardable seconds) became a popular Craftsman-style masonry choice; it was also used to good effect on towering chimneys (SEE FIGURE 39). Often, a house with shingled walls or other wood siding had porch columns, a chimney, and a foundation of brick or stone (SEE FIGURES 10, 41–43, 54 AND 62). In particular, stone was a naturally expressive choice for the Craftsman style. Many varieties were used, with rounded river rock (cobble) among the most popular. Generally, most were chosen from whatever type was most easily available, and often quarried locally. Using randomly placed combinations of both brick and stone, striking textural effects (then nicknamed "the peanut brittle style") could also be achieved (SEE FIGURE 39–40). Whatever masonry treatment might be used for the porch columns would most likely be repeated on the chimney. In many other examples, porch columns were made entirely of wood: square in plan, but frequently trapezoidal in their elevation, with gently tapering sides supported below by a wider rectangular base (or pier) that tied into the porch railing.

Figure 41.

HOUSE IN SAN DIEGO, CALIFORNIA (CA. 1910).

With its weighty, substantial feeling, this Mission Hills-area home exudes the solidity of the Craftsman style. Supported by four tapering columns of river rock matched on the chimney, the full-width front porch is asymmetrically composed of a forward-facing gable offset toward the left. The front walkway through its right half is still centered on the house. Also matching the shallow pitch of the main roof, a pair of side-facing gables completes the porch roof's form. Supported on projecting purlins (beams) and large brackets set to either side, the primary gable's eaves overshadow a shed-roof awning above the central second-story windows. Exposed rafter tails make a rhythmic march down the side of the house.

Figure 43.

WEAVER HOUSE IN SPOKANE, WASHINGTON (1910).

With a skillfully executed and well-scaled design, this large, shingled, Craftsman-style home, designed by local architect Alfred Jones, literally adapts one of the most familiar of the overall forms that were applied to many smaller bungalows. With a side-facing gable orientation, its sweeping, oversized roof extends forward over the front porch; a forward-facing dormer above contains the original screened-in sleeping porch. Its full two-story plan also includes a basement and a roomy third-floor attic level, contributing more usable space. Exhibiting particularly well-detailed clinker brickwork, the front porch has arched openings around its foundation level. Given more visibility than most, a secondary side entrance (through the red door seen at left) leads to a vestibule lined with original leaded-glass windows.

Figure 42.

WILBUR-HAHN HOUSE IN SPOKANE, WASHINGTON (1916).

Facing a downhill slope, the stunning rear façade of this Craftsman-style house happens to be its most imposing one. Designed by noted local architect Kirtland Cutter, the house was completed in collaboration with his associate, G.A. Pehrson. Entered from the opposite uphill side, the house appears much lower and smaller from that perspective. An extravagant use of stone, the local volcanic basalt, on both the home's exterior walls and for the enormous tapering columns and attached "arcades" (to the left) gives this design monumental strength. Its compelling connection to the landscape is reinforced by the presence of many naturally occurring boulders (foreground) on the property. Hung with original period lanterns, the long, covered rear porch adjoining the main living level is beautifully sheltered. On this side of the house, the basement includes some well-lit living spaces at ground level that open directly onto a covered patio area.

Figure 44.

FRONT DOOR OF THE WEAVER HOUSE IN FIGURE 43.

Revealed behind an original oak screen door, a stylistic tour de force of original Arts and Crafts metalwork adorns this front door. Taking its design cue from a circular window, an otherwise plain slab door is veneered in quartersawn oak, and sheets of brass have been fashioned into strap hinges quite fancifully interpreted. However, their spiky outlines and curling ends betray some debt to Gothic-style metalwork, an English influence, in harmony with the diamond-paned, leaded-glass sidelights. A pair of handsome period sconces completes this ensemble.

Figure 45. (opposite)

LIVING ROOM OF THE MERRILL HOUSE (FIGURE 45).

The front door opens into the entry hall seen at left, with a separate dining room off to the far left. This spacious living room is accessed by passing under a full-width, second-floor balcony. An open screen wall of thick, squared columns with low display cabinets built in between each pair, supports the balcony. Vaulted into a peak that reflects the actual roofline, the beamed ceiling is lit by the original chandelier. The ceiling's pitch turns slightly shallow above the balcony, where it transitions into the differently angled two-story portion of the house. Fully paneled up to a high plate rail, the living room is divided into different sitting areas and is mostly furnished with Arts and Crafts-period furniture. One of its many intriguing features, the living room's focal point is its fireplace, set in a low-ceilinged inglenook lined with built-in benches. To the left of the inglenook, French doors open to the front porch.

Figure 46.

J. B. MERRILL HOUSE, LOS ANGELES, CALIFORNIA (1908).

Local architect H. M. Patterson designed the angled form of this home in response to the sloping contours of its Mount Washington neighborhood site. Faced with extra-long wood shingles, the streetside façade is dominated by a two-story section, with three distinctive louvered vents arranged in its upper gable, and wooden flower boxes supported on corbels under its second-story windows. A pair of square, clinker brick columns support the shed roof of the entry porch and frame the front door. The pitch of the entry-porch roof is repeated on the single-story roof of the angled wing that ends in a side-facing gable to the left. The entry porch adjoins a longer covered front-porch area, with French doors opening into the living room. Guarded by a cat, the curving front path is of herringbone-patterned brick.

A famous tenet of the Arts and Crafts movement, applied to everything from furniture to entire buildings, is that the structural forms needed to hold things together should be seen, thereby expressed as an integral element of a design's overall beauty. This concept of revealed construction was particularly prevalent in Craftsman-style architecture. One of the most common examples of the idea may be seen in the large brackets (knee braces) routinely positioned beneath the roof's deeply overhanging eaves, which contribute a sense of support and sturdiness to the design. Sometimes variations of this concept alternately employed large projecting roof beams (purlins) that extended beneath the eaves. Pairs (or a series) of similar but smaller-scale supporting brackets (corbels) might be placed beneath shallower roof projections or used as supports under windowsills and flower boxes.

Another easily recognizable Craftsman-style detail employs some variation of the mortise and tenon, a feature far more typical on Arts and Crafts furniture, in which a length of wood (tenon) is tightly fitted (mortised) through an opening in another length of wood. To hold a tenon in place, a small, elongated wedge-shaped piece of wood (key) is passed completely through the tenon. Derived from much earlier furniture-making traditions going back to the medieval period, this method of joinery was originally conceived as a way for furniture to be easily taken apart for moving or storage, and then put back together when needed by pulling the key out, or pushing it back in. For example, long trestle tables and their benches, otherwise both cumbersome to move, often employed this detail in their medieval construction.

For such a relatively refined detail to be adequately visible on a Craftsman home's exterior, its scale had to be much larger than similar detailing on furniture (SEE FIGURES 38 AND 151). Despite the incongruity with Arts and Crafts principles, some structural elements are not always what they appear to be. To achieve the Craftsman look, many architects and builders simply applied facsimiles of such elements to masquerade as the real thing.

WHITE PINES AND THE BYRDCLIFFE COLONY,
WOODSTOCK, NEW YORK (1903)

White Pines was built as the home of Ralph Radcliffe Whitehead (1854–1929) and his wife, Jane Byrd McCall Whitehead (1861–1955), who were the founders of the important Arts and Crafts colony called Byrdcliffe (an adaptation of their middle names). Although not a trained architect, Whitehead worked out the plan and design of their home with help from Bolton Brown (1862–1936), an artist and early participant in the Byrdcliffe venture. Whitehead was a well-to-do Englishman who studied with John Ruskin at Oxford, and later met William Morris. He relocated to America after marrying Jane Byrd McCall in 1892. Coming from an affluent Philadelphia family, she had first met Ralph in 1885 while studying painting in Europe. Although the home was a collaboration with her husband, Jane made her own creative contributions to White Pines. Unusual for Arts and Crafts proponents at the time, the Whiteheads' affluence obviated the need to work for a living, so they divided their time between Woodstock and a winter home in Montecito, California. Their means and mobility brought them an unusual perspective on America's Arts and Crafts movement, as well as contact with many of its most notable proponents. Prior to their Byrdcliffe venture, they resided on a large Montecito estate they had built in 1894 called Arcady. On this property they opened a small Sloyd School in 1898, which employed a Swedish technique to teach manual training with an emphasis on woodworking that resonated with Arts and Crafts ideals. Despite their wealth, they craved the simple, meaningful life extolled by Ruskin and Morris. By 1901, after their two sons were born, they sought a place to raise them that would also fulfill their ongoing dream of founding a community inspired by Arts and Crafts principles. Founded in 1902, The Byrdcliffe colony began to produce handcrafted furniture, pottery, and textiles, but it was never profitable enough to be self-sufficient. This factor and other personal conflicts of the Whiteheads with their collaborators contributed to the colony's closure by 1906. But the Whiteheads stayed on at White Pines, continuing their own crafts pursuits. Other arts-oriented endeavors evolved in and around Byrdcliffe and Woodstock over time, securing an artistic reputation for the area that still persists and thrives.

The legacy did not continue with the Whiteheads' two sons, Ralph Jr. (1899–1928) and Peter (1901–1976). Not pursuing his parents' interests, Ralph Jr. was unstable as a youth, but had settled down to engineering work in South America. After a visit home, he was headed back there when his boat sank near the Bahamas and he perished. His heartbroken father died a few months later. Although trained in several fields, Peter eschewed a working career and remained at Byrdcliffe with his mother; White Pines remained his primary lifelong residence. He willed most of the Byrdcliffe property to the Woodstock Guild, but left White Pines to a great-nephew of his mother. In 1999, the house was purchased by the Woodstock Guild, which reunited it with the other remaining Byrdcliffe properties.

Today, under the auspices of the Woodstock Guild (its official steward and present owner), the wooded landscape of the Byrdcliffe Arts Colony, and the exteriors of twenty-eight surviving original buildings, may be viewed on self-guided walking tours. White Pines may also be visited on pre-arranged, guided group tours.

Figure 47. (opposite)
STAIR HALL AT WHITE PINES.

Warmly welcoming, this area's natural wood and exposed structural elements have an austere elegance. The use of low risers on the staircase contributes to its graceful proportions. A period Byrdcliffe piece, the table by the stairs features through-tenon detailing. The Whiteheads' tall-case clock on the stair landing is seen in the same location in period photographs. Next to a secondary outside door, a window seat with an angled back and spindled arms resembles a piece of furniture. The open closet under the stairs was once screened by a portière (doorway drapery); the arched door at right leads to rear utility areas and a service stair. This entry hall continues further to the right, connecting to the dining room and other service areas in a wide, gallerylike extension. From the square column at center, toward the back wall, the ceiling is open to the second floor, where open railings repeat the simple design of the staircase. From the second-floor stair hall, a separately placed, open flight of stairs along the wall at right rises to the attic-level White Pines Pottery studio. By choosing to live in such proximity to their artistic pursuits, the Whiteheads achieved an Arts and Crafts ideal, albeit with live-in servants under the same roof.

Figure 48.

WHITE PINES, BYRDCLIFFE COLONY, WOODSTOCK, NEW YORK (1903).

Other Byrdcliffe buildings adapted the simple style and materials of White Pines. The use of local stone, unpainted wood, plain detailing, and exposed structural elements reflects a more progressive, West Coast, Craftsman sensibility. The asymmetrical composition of the house includes both gabled and hipped forms in its roof. Above the front porch is an enclosed sleeping porch. The shed-roofed bay at right was a later addition. The notch in the eaves at left allowed more light into Jane Whitehead's bedroom, while the upper front gable and tiny attic dormer window mark the location of the White Pines Pottery Studio. Nearly half of the first and second floors of White Pines were planned as living space for servants or for their household duties. The low stone walls in front once framed lawn and garden areas, though sweeping views of the countryside are now obscured by overgrown woods.

> The Whiteheads craved the simple, meaningful life extolled by Ruskin and Morris.

Figure 49.

DINING ROOM AT WHITE PINES.

Located at the right front corner of the house, the dining room is simply detailed. The folding screen at left, handpainted with a map of the Byrdcliffe colony, dates to the 1930s. It covers part of a built-in buffet, which abuts an offset blue-painted brick fireplace with a built-in bench on the right. Low-relief fleur-de-lis motifs are carved into the chair backs and table supports of original oak Byrdcliffe dining furniture. This room's original relationship to adjacent rooms to the left was altered in later years. Now opened into one large space, these areas share a window-lined, shed-roofed bay added on the façade's first floor that appears in a 1918 photograph. Original door openings that lead from the stair hall to these front-room spaces, including the dining room, were reduced to a single door, and window placements were rearranged.

Figure 50.

LIVING ROOM AT WHITE PINES.

Open to the entry hall, the living room, called the "Pine Tree Room" by the Whiteheads, is at the front left corner of the house. The simple built-in features recall Japanese cabinetry. A 1909 photograph of this room taken by Jessie Tarbox Beals shows this orange burlap wall treatment, as well as the metal incense burner on the mantel. The pottery pieces were made in the pottery studio upstairs. The hand-selected, handmade ceramic tiles on the fireplace have irregular green glazing, tinged with orange, with two tiles displaying Ralph Whitehead's initials (RRW). The tile border and andirons feature the fleur-de-lis motif, the logo of the Byrdcliffe colony and the Whiteheads' personal emblem. Jane's cousin, Henry Chapman Mercer, made these tiles at his Moravian Pottery and Tileworks at Doylestown, Pennsylvania (SEE FIGURE 126).

Figure 51. (right)

BRIDGE TO THE LOOM ROOM (ADDED TO WHITE PINES, 1906).

A covered, window-lined footbridge was added by Ralph Whitehead to allow direct access from his home to the new Loom Room, a workroom built next door and dedicated to textile weaving. By the time of its construction, the Byrdcliffe colony had already disbanded. From the interior of White Pines, on the servant's side of the house, the bridge was planned so that it could be entered through the back of a large linen storage closet, lined with built-in cabinetry. The view behind and to the right of White Pines shows the site's uphill slope that the construction had to accommodate. As with their pottery studio in the attic, the Whiteheads' direct linking of their home to this workspace reflected an unusual personal commitment to their craft pursuits.

Figure 52.

INTERIOR OF THE LOOM ROOM.

The Loom Room is brightly lit by several skylights along the north side of its peaked roof, as White Pines did not have electricity until 1914. The room was heated by a large, plaster-faced fireplace (out of view). Above a square mantel, incised into a sloping hooded form, is one of the Whiteheads' favorite quotations in Greek from Sophocles' Ajax. On the plaster face of the chimney is a large fleur-de-lis motif set in a diamond-shaped frame. Once used in the colony's library, the long center table is a Byrdcliffe period piece and features low-relief carvings of stylized flowers down its legs. The door on the right side is the front outside entrance to the Loom Room.

Figure 53.

BEDROOM AT WHITE PINES.

This room located directly above the dining room may have been used by the Whiteheads' sons, Ralph Jr. and Peter, when they were young children. The restrained design of the built-in bench and attached dresser are detailed similar to the cabinetry seen on the first floor. The façade's large, front-facing gable determined the clipped angle of the ceiling above the far wall; part of its eaves are visible outside the windows. The window above the bench overlooks the Loom Room.

As photos in this chapter confirm, the interiors of larger Craftsman-style homes offer many more opportunities for classic Arts and Crafts expressions. As was true with the bungalow, the best place to look for these are in a home's primary public rooms, where the greater part of the interior design budget was generally allocated. In larger homes, special features such as vaulted or cathedral ceiling con figurations are more likely to be found (SEE FIGURE 64). Millwork and its detailing are another important aspect of Arts and Crafts expression. Some larger homes feature less-common varieties of wood for the paneling and the inevitable built-in cabinetry, with accordingly more refined detailing used in their assembly. Fireplaces are often a home's most stunning focal point, many with exceptional tile surrounds or an extravagant use of stone (SEE FIGURES 40, 49, 55 AND 63); inglenooks (recessed alcoves with a fireplace and built-in seating) are always desirable features (SEE FIGURE 45), and stairways, typically unseen in bungalows, were also widely interpreted as design elements (SEE FIGURES 47 AND 59).

Craftsman Revival

In recent years, a sweeping reevaluation of Craftsman-style homes across America helped recover much of the long-faded glory of its original, progressive design context. From the distance of our current perspective, a newfound reverence for the style's signature use of natural materials and its characteristic features is growing. Drawn to them for these reasons, many homeowners of vintage Craftsman homes are turning out to be excellent stewards of these historic treasures, caring for them with a commitment and sensitivity not seen since they were first built. Today's Arts and Crafts revival helps foster new awareness of what to do (and what not to do) with these old houses when contemplating remodels or additions. The style's renaissance has also spawned an entirely new generation of Craftsman homes: those that are newly built from the ground up. It seems Gustav Stickley's vision is alive and well.

Figure 55.

LIVING ROOM OF THE DEEPHAVEN HOUSE (FIGURE 54).

Beneath a ceiling of closely spaced box beams and dominated by a fireplace with an overscaled surround of matte-glazed, green Grueby tile, the living room forms the heart of this home's gathering space; all other rooms radiate out from here. An inset panel of ten large landscape tiles, with designs visible as raised outlines, are glazed in a matching color against a field of plain tiles above the fireplace opening. To the left of the mantel is a row of built-in bookcases with glass doors; to the right is a slatted screen and built-in bench. The stairs behind these terminate in a full-height, octagonal column with carved foliated ornament at its top. Beyond the stairs, the front door adjoins a hallway to the kitchen, placed on the inland side of this lakeside house; the dining room is toward the far left. An eclectic touch, classical antiquity provides the motif of crossing lines in the doors and windows. Unusually ornate for a Craftsman style interior, the large carved corbels of the fireplace mantel may have been salvaged from the earlier Victorian-era home that this house replaced.

Figure 54.

HOUSE IN DEEPHAVEN, MINNESOTA (CA. 1905).

During the nineteenth century, Lake Minnetonka became a popular site for summer homes such as this one, as well as sprawling resort hotels. This view shows the ground-hugging posture of the two-story Craftsman-style home on its lakeside façade. Its inland side, with a proper upright posture and a restrained composition, differs considerably. On a high foundation of randomly sized stones, the structure nestles into its sloping site. Down a steeply descending path and stairs at right, an original boathouse sits at the water's edge. Sprawling glassed-in sun porches surround three sides of the first floor. At center, deep overhangs and a low-slung gable shelter a recessed open sitting area. The present owner meticulously restored all of this home's badly weathered exterior elements, and its walls, windows, and hundreds of decoratively shaped rafter tails are now all aglow in warm, period-appropriate paint colors.

Figure 56.

DINING ROOM OF THE DEEPHAVEN HOUSE.

This view of the dining room is from the doorway to the living room. A built-in sideboard and a pair of doors at right interpret the Craftsman style in quartersawn oak. A closet door is near the corner, while a swinging door to the right opens to the kitchen. The dining room ceiling's box beams are turned ninety degrees from those in the living room. Both the wall sconces and the combination gas-and-electric chandelier over the dining table are period pieces. On the opposite side of the house as that seen in Figure 55, another sunporch sitting area is visible through the far doorway. On the wall across from the sideboard, a set of French doors and windows overlooks the lake.

Figure 57.

SUNPORCH OF THE DEEPHAVEN HOUSE.

This view of one of the back corners of the house shows finishes and detailing that are common to all of the porch areas. Seen from the direction of the covered open porch area seen in Figure 54, the lake view is toward the left, and the dining room is through the doorway at right. In an otherwise fully painted environment, the natural wood finish of the bead-board ceilings adds warmth and character. Oversized, double-hung, multipaned windows line all the exterior walls of the porches, substantially extending seasonal usage in an area known for its harsh winters. They also serve as an extra insulating buffer against colder weather. With an abundance of appropriate places to use it, the owner has become an avid collector of period wicker furniture.

Figure 58.

THE MARSTON HOUSE, SAN DIEGO, CALIFORNIA (1905).

Built for George W. and Anna Marston , this 8,500-square-foot house is sited on four acres of gardens, now part of the western edge of Balboa Park. Marston was an active philanthropist with many civic-minded pursuits. Important progressive architect Irving J. Gill, then of the San Diego firm of Hebbard and Gill, was the designer. The main entrance to the house is beneath a porte-cochère, which extends from the far left end. A raised terrace adjoins the dining room and the garden, and is anchored by a glass-windowed, garden pavilion at right, whose upswept eaves hint at an Oriental influence. Shed-roof dormers and large knee braces (brackets) under the eaves are Craftsman-style elements. In 1974, the original family's eldest daughter, Mary Marston, bequeathed the house and its gardens to the San Diego Historical Society. Both house and garden are open to the public.

Figure 59.

ENTRY AND STAIR HALL OF THE MARSTON HOUSE.

Gill envisioned a clear, straightforward plan: a central circulation space that bisected the first floor length-wise, and extended from the front door at far left to the dining room at the opposite end. Breaking up its considerable length, the main stairway is placed opposite a wide doorway into the living room. At this point, the linear hallway dissolves into a wider, cross-axial space, reinforced by the strong lines of woodwork elements, that draws the eye's attention from side to side. The staircase incorporates low risers for a gentler ascent, and a generous built-in bench that faces the living room fireplace, a built-in storage cabinet with a usable top shelf, and an elegant assembly of substantial square posts and spindles. Daylight enters the area from the south-facing living room and from the band of windows that parallels the staircase at the second floor.

Figure 60.

DINING ROOM OF THE MARSTON HOUSE.

The built-in sideboard in this well-lit dining room backs a butler's pantry, which is reached through the swinging door near the corner. The back center panel of the sideboard was designed as a convenient pass-through. The quartersawn oak finish is matched in the recently crafted, Craftsman-style dining furniture. French doors frame the simple elegance of the brick and painted-steel fireplace. To the right, a series of French doors and windows, with matching detailing in their upper sashes, opens onto a brick terrace with a garden pavilion (seen in Figure 58), with steps leading into the garden. This south-facing room looks over an expansive lawn backed by tall trees. On the far side of the house are more formally planned gardens, including a teahouse, viewing pergola, and fountain that were added in the 1920s.

Figure 61.

LIBRARY OF THE MARSTON HOUSE.

This is one of the first two rooms encountered upon entering the home; across the hall is a smaller music room that opens to the living room. As is consistent throughout this house, the millwork detailing is simply and beautifully detailed without an ounce of pretension. A welcoming and comfortable front corner space, the room is lined with built-in bookcases housing the Marstons' original library. Proximity to the front door made this a convenient and private place for George Marston to conduct business meetings without disturbing other family members. Many of the furnishings seen today in the Marston house belonged to the family. The fireplace sits opposite the left-hand window. The wall finish, a painted texture over a grasscloth like material, replicates the original.

Figure 62.

F. A. THOMAS HOUSE, BERKELEY, CALIFORNIA (1911).

Located in the Northbrae neighborhood, this home was designed by Julia Morgan (1872–1957), the most famous woman architect of the Arts and Crafts period and the first woman graduate of the prestigious Ecole des Beaux Arts in Paris, the most esteemed place to study architecture at the time. She is best known as the architect of the monumental Hearst Castle (La Cuesta Encantada) in San Simeon, California. The major portion of the Thomas house is comprised of two side-facing gables penetrated by a large forward-facing dormer, which creates a full second floor in that portion. The dormer's distinctive triple-gable effect largely defines the roofline. Out of view to the left, with a side-facing gable on its far end, a single-story wing houses a vaulted-ceiling living room. A covered porch extends fully across the front of the house, and an open outdoor terrace parallels the living room wing in a continuation of the porch. Inside and out, the Thomas house features a locally quarried stone known as Northbrae rhyolite, which is used impressively in the porch and terrace railing walls, square columns and foundation, front stairs, and the extensive retaining walls.

Figure 63. (opposite)

LIVING ROOM OF THE THOMAS HOUSE.

Easily the most impressive room in the house, the living room is a testimony to the warm beauty of natural heart redwood as an interior finish material. A refined version of an Arts and Crafts tenet of revealed construction, the ceiling is artistically detailed with diagonally placed planks, creating a large-scale version of the herringbone pattern between its beams and cross braces. Such angled sheathing is also an effective way to increase seismic stability. The room's peaked form reflects the roof of its single-story wing. Upon entry, a towering stone fireplace and chimney of Northbrae rhyolite commands the far wall. At right, French doors open directly to a sheltered patio and the rear garden. Salvaged from a San Francisco home, the period sideboard at right, acquired at auction by the homeowners, was once an original built-in feature.

Figure 64.

LIVING ROOM (TOWARD ENTRY HALL) OF THE THOMAS HOUSE.

This view helps explain the living room's spatial relationship to the rest of the house. The French doors open to the entry hall paneled in quartersawn oak. The front door is to the right. The dining room and library are partly visible through a doorway beyond. To the left, the staircase rises to the second floor of the main part of the house (note the rounded lower step protruding into the doorway). The breakfast room, kitchen, and service areas are along the back side of the house and are accessible from the dining room and library. Above the French doors, a second-floor balcony with a square-spindled railing, supported on stepped corbels, overlooks the room. As possibly a "musicians' gallery," it also aids in air circulation for the high-ceilinged space. Arch-topped windows at right face an open terrace along the front.

In recent years, a sweeping reevaluation of Craftsman-style homes across America helped recover much of the long-faded glory of its original, progressive design context.

Figure 65.

DINING ROOM OF THE THOMAS HOUSE.

Intimately scaled, the dining room is paneled entirely in heart redwood. Because it was designed to be viewed at a much closer range than in the living room, the detailing has a more delicate and refined character. Utilizing wide redwood planks rather than beams, the ceiling is finished in the same board-and-batten style as the living room walls. Mitered crown molding lends a traditional effect to the room's perimeter, and cross-banding around the room creates the effect of a plain wooden frieze. The compact diagonal corner fireplace has a matte-glazed ceramic-tile surround in harmony with the tones of the wood and rug. Through the doorway on the far wall, the library is lined with built-in bookcases with an adaptation of a period landscape frieze design fitted into the space above. The mix of furniture periods in these rooms shows the adaptability and versatility of a simple Arts and Crafts style home.

Figure 66.

GAMBLE HOUSE, PASADENA, CALIFORNIA (1908).

The Gamble House is one of the most famous of all American Arts and Crafts homes. David and Mary Gamble, retiring from the family business Procter & Gamble, commissioned the firm of Greene and Greene to design their Pasadena home. The Gamble house is so well-scaled and proportioned that its considerable size becomes secondary to its satisfying composition. This design is made to appear more modest through its assemblage of "readable" parts, breaking up the perception of mass. Open terraces and sleeping porches reduce the home's visual weight with movements of light and shadow, contrasting voids against solids. Centrally, the second floor overhangs the first, reducing the effect of mass with shadow lines. The portion with the forward-facing gable at left, along with the prominent raised terrace across the front, tethers the whole composition to the ground. A horizontal emphasis suggests the house is lower than it is; the third floor's height is suppressed into the second floor's roof. There is also a subtle Oriental influence most often cited as Japanese. With its architect-designed furnishings still in place, the interior is equally compelling. The Gamble House is open to the public as a house museum.

Figure 67.

GRAY HOUSE, LOS ANGELES, CALIFORNIA (1909).

Pasadena architect Alfred Heineman, known for his skill at manipulating Craftsman-style forms into creative compositions, designed the Gray House. It cost $8,600 to build, considerably beyond the average budget. That same year, Alfred began collaborating with his brother Arthur, who was a local building contractor. The basic form of this house, a two-story rectangular box, has been augmented at its roofline by two separate gabled forms. The dominant, forward-facing gable is slightly higher, allowing a graceful overlapping of roof eaves with the side-facing gable. In a striking detail seen on other Heineman-designed houses, a cantilevered, canopylike roof structure shelters the front door. Resting on long, outstretched brackets, it receives supplemental support at its center peak from a heavy chain attached higher up on the building's façade. Screened by foliage and a low, brick-capped stucco wall, a slightly raised open-air terrace fronts the building. Windows line a large screened porch beneath the side-facing gable. Directly above the first floor's painted stucco-faced walls, the second floor's shingled walls are flared out, a detail that sheds water away from the building.

CRAFTSMAN CROSSOVERS, PART I:
ROMANTIC TO EXOTIC INFLUENCES

Swiss Chalet Style

ARTS AND CRAFTS—PERIOD HOMES in the Swiss Chalet style are among the earliest of any that combine a different styles' characteristic design elements with those of the Craftsman style. Generally, these two styles make a fairly seamless pairing and in some examples it may be unclear at first where one style influence ends and the other begins. In a closer look, most of these particular crossover homes have enough of the signature features most often associated with the Swiss Chalet that their European ancestry is fairly obvious. More than with most other styles, the Swiss Chalet's early-twentieth-century influence has been reinterpreted and often somewhat romanticized in many later versions, most frequently for vacation homes in mountain ski-resort areas.

One feature common to most of these homes is the extensive use of wood on their exteriors, usually left unpainted. Some feature exterior walls on the first-floor level painted a light color (SEE FIGURES 69 AND 72), which function as a kind of visual pedestal for the wood-faced second-floor and attic levels, where most of the home's design interest is typically concentrated. After all, these homes

Figure 68.

POSTCARD VIEW OF "A HILLSIDE RESIDENCE IN SOUTHERN CALIFORNIA" (CA. 1910).

Because of its mountainous backdrop and hillside siting, the Swiss Chalet influence seems more pronounced, despite the subtropical plantings. Swiss Chalet influence is visible in the gable to the right in the use of carving or turning along the oversized brackets that support the deep eaves. Anchored by a large stone chimney, the overall composition shows Craftsman-style influence with its two prominent gables; most Swiss Chalet homes rely on one forward-facing gable to make their style statement. Although this example makes more literal references to a Swiss Chalet than most, the similarly woodsy style of the earliest Craftsman homes in the Pasadena area was, for a time, nicknamed "Japo-Swiss." This house survives intact today although vegetation now obscures its visibility.

Figure 69.

LANG HOUSE IN SPOKANE, WASHINGTON (CA. 1910).

Surrounded by greenery, this home's setting in the South Hill district make a convincing case for its Swiss Chalet style. It was designed by prominent local architect Kirtland Cutter. Finely detailed, decorative wooden elements are delicate, relative to the home's larger scale. Notable are the roof's narrow, scallop-edged fascia boards, patterned cuts in the edging below the attic window, small brackets of stepped form, larger stepped brackets under the eaves, and the balcony railing's cutout design. Less typical are the curving brackets supporting the balcony. The roof's clipped (jerkin-headed) gable is less typical but of European lineage. On the side, the shed-roof dormer configuration permits a full second floor, while allowing the lowered eaves of the front gable to preserve the design's ground-hugging posture. The first floor's lightly painted stucco walls also reduce the home's apparent height.

were originally designed for alpine settings, with their façades best viewed from the perspective of a downhill slope. Used to express different floor levels, the wood siding of a Swiss Chalet home may vary in type, width, and linear direction, on the same house. For example, horizontal clapboard siding on the first floor is frequently offset by vertical siding (sometimes board-and-batten style) on the second floor or attic level (SEE FIGURES 70 AND 71).

Besides a lot of wood, the most significant feature of a Swiss Chalet is the prominent form of its roof, which also closely parallels some examples of the Craftsman style. Almost invariably, Swiss Chalets are characterized by a dominant, forward-facing gable whose eaves are extended forward, creating a deep, sheltering overhang in front. In most examples, this overhang largely supplants the usual need of a first-floor front porch. The angled pitch of the roof is usually fairly steep to shed snow, and the eaves on either side of the façade also extend quite deeply beyond the side walls. In some cases, the roof incorporates a clipped (jerkin-headed) gable, a traditional detail common to other European sources, including the English Cottage (SEE FIGURE 69). In crossover homes with more Craftsman than Swiss Chalet elements, shingled walls may be used (at least on the first-floor level), and open wooden truss work, appearing more structural than decorative in effect, may also be set into the peaked eaves of their front gables (SEE FIGURE 73).

Although most Swiss Chalet–style homes are a full two stories, the second floor often appears somewhat smaller than it really is, due to the lowering effect of the sides' extended roof eaves, which can appear to dip almost to the top of the first-floor level (SEE FIGURES 69 AND 70). Separate from its effects on the front façade, another element incorporated into some Swiss Chalet roofs are side dormers. These tend to be of the shed-roof variety, and although by necessity set at a slightly different pitch, most are wide enough to still appear well integrated with the lines of the roof. While such dormers add additional usable space to the upper levels of the house, their effect on its apparent outward size ends up being fairly minimal. The deep roof eaves also further shield the side dormers' visibility.

Figure 71.

House in Spokane, Washington (1911).

This home's appealing Swiss Chalet style is enhanced by its secluded site and forested setting. It was designed and built by Karl Koerner as his own residence. A projecting front terrace, now shaded by a canvas awning, is detailed in Craftsman style. Substantial, battered (sloping) stone columns secure the outside corners and serve as posts for the wooden railings, which have typical cutout motifs in their boards that repeat on the second-floor balcony. Less typical, the encircling balcony gives the house horizontal emphasis, and fosters indoor-outdoor living from its upstairs rooms. The fascia boards on the front gable are detailed at their ends with curving flourishes cut into the lower edges. The uphill siting shows off the deeply stepped brackets beneath the gable's eaves. At right, similar brackets are seen supporting the balcony and flanking a flowerpot shelf under the living room window. Vertical siding on the upper gable walls switches to horizontal on the lower levels.

Figure 70. (opposite)

Frank Alva Jacobs House, Portland, Oregon (1913).

This Mount Tabor district home is the only known residential project by the firm of Johnson and Mayer. The house is sited below street level with views of the city from the back. The living and dining rooms are oriented toward the city view, and open onto a raised terrace. Carefully composed, typical Swiss Chalet elements articulate its simple form, the front-facing gable faced in vertical board-and-batten siding being most prominent. Supported on deep brackets shaped by curving edges, a wide balcony has access from two bedrooms across the front. Trimmed by fascia boards (bargeboards) with scalloped edges, the roof extends lower on the far right. Horizontal lines dominate the first floor walls, which rest on a stone foundation. The front door is off the open porch on the right. The house has more than 4,300 square feet, including walk-out basement rooms to the garden level in the back.

Figure 72.

HOUSE IN SPOKANE, WASHINGTON (CA. 1915).

One of the striking vestiges of the South Hill district geologic past is the house-sized volcanic basalt boulder (locally known as a "haystack" outcropping) at right. The boulder makes this roomy house appear almost doll-house size. Further reducing its apparent size is the white-painted, stucco-faced first floor, which limits the visually heavier natural wood siding (all placed in a horizontal direction) to the upper one-and-a-half stories. The front door vestibule and a bay window extend forward to support a deep, second-floor balcony. The balcony narrows as it wraps around the sides of the house. Typical of the Swiss Chalet style, the flower boxes add color and the home is sheltered beneath a deeply overhanging roof with a forward-facing gable. Hanging from scalloped-edge fascia boards are pendantlike trim pieces, each aligned with a stepped bracket under the eaves. The attic balcony suggests more usable living space on the third floor.

Figure 73.

HOUSE IN MILWAUKEE, WISCONSIN (CA. 1900).

The Swiss Chalet style is interpreted here in a late Victorian-era home. The wood elements are more delicately scaled, and are painted, instead of finished naturally. Elements such as the exposed rafter tails are placed as if structural, but are generally decorative stylizations. Similarly, the exposed truss work adds interest but little structure in the upper gable; its purpose seems mainly to display the triangular panel insets of lacy decoration in perforated wood. Thin, sticklike brackets support the truss and a shallow balcony, which extends further back into an arched attic-level recess. The railing of cutout boards, and the vertical siding in the upper gable with zigzag detailing, are in the Swiss Chalet tradition. The Craftsman style appears in the simple shed-roof over the front porch, its plain supporting posts, and its square, spindled railings.

Figure 74.

COVER OF BUNGALOW MAGAZINE (1910).

Adapted from Buddhist-temple structures found in China and Japan, this interpretation of the pagoda form on the cover of the January 1910 Bungalow Magazine *is more literal than most in the Craftsman era. While not a typical interpretation, it was the design for an actual house, and an accompanying article in the issue included its floor plans. Erroneously, it was called "a Japanese Torri." A torii is a ceremonial gateway of a Japanese temple compound. The article described a house of this design as having been built in Jamaica, New York, "for Miss Blanche Sloan, the actress, whose artistic temperament required a summer house that not only provides all of the requirements of occidental life, but also embodies much of the refinement that is invariably present in the architecture of the land of the Mikado." To allow Miss Sloan to practice on the trapeze, the third level was left as open space. The magazine was used as a marketing tool for the plan book designs of Los Angeles architect Henry L. Wilson. It is known that as early as 1905, a similar house (known locally as the Bungoda) had been built in Biscayne Bay, Florida.*

The façade of a Swiss Chalet–style home may be likened to that of a cuckoo clock, a helpful analogy when envisioning its characteristic features and demeanor. A particularly common feature is a wide balcony across the second-floor level, with a fairly shallow projection supported on brackets or extended beams. Along with the deep roof eaves, this balcony also provides some degree of shelter for the point of entry on the first floor below. Occasionally, a second, smaller, balcony also occurs on the third-floor attic level. A particular railing style common to their balconies is a definitive detail of most Swiss Chalets. In lieu of conventional spindles, plain wide boards are set vertically, edge-to-edge, with very narrow gaps between. What animates the effect of this otherwise low and nearly solid railing into such a signature feature is the introduction of strategically placed cutouts along each side edge of the boards. The cutouts in each board are then aligned in mirror image with those on the adjacent boards, resulting in a repeating, overall decorative pattern along the length of the railing. Depending on the shapes of these cutouts, railing patterns could vary from softer effects using circles and curves, to bolder, geometric ones using angular lines, or a combination of both.

The ornamental nature of their balcony railings reinforces the cuckoo clock analogy, for there is a calculated tendency on Swiss Chalet–style homes to impart a picturesque effect. In some actual Swiss and other European examples, woodwork elements may also be decorated with painted or stenciled decoration. Most American versions are fairly sedate, but still usually less austere than most Craftsman-style homes.

Swiss Chalet–style homes may feature linear geometric carving applied to some structural elements, such as projecting beam ends, rafter tails, or brackets. Alternately, the edges of these may be simply chamfered (beveled). Another area of decorative potential are fascia boards (bargeboards), used to cover the narrow edges of the front-facing eaves, which are usually wide enough to allow some motif or pattern to be cut into their face. This may be a curving scalloped motif, which can

occur either along the fascia boards' entire length, or be limited to specific parts of them. Popular warm-weather accents for almost any interpretation of a Swiss Chalet are flower-filled window boxes.

Another signature feature of most Swiss Chalets are the correspondingly deep brackets (corbels) that extend beneath their eaves to the fascia boards, working in tandem with the exaggerated roof overhangs. While some of these may resemble the form of typical Craftsman-style knee braces (brackets), the most distinctive and robust examples are those comprised of multiple wood beams sandwiched together to form a single oversized bracket in the form of inverted steps. Occasionally, a similarly stepped bracket at a much smaller scale is paired with square Craftsman-style porch posts, lending more visual support for the beam above. Extra interest is added to the posts' plain silhouette by their stepped form. Swiss Chalet designs may incorporate brackets of more than one size, corresponding to the varying requirements of different areas on the house. For greater emphasis, the balcony's supporting brackets may be given a different design than the others, for they are more likely to be seen at closer range, from the ground.

Early-twentieth-century versions of the Swiss Chalet style became linked to progressive design. As a significant influence on bungalows, it was adapted in plan-book house designs, and written about in many places, including Gustav Stickley's the *Craftsman* magazine, and Henry Saylor's book *Bungalows* (1911). Creative interpretations of Swiss Chalets figured rather prominently in the earlier work of noted northern California architect Bernard Maybeck (SEE FIGURE 110–112), and by others in the Bay Area's "First Bay Tradition" period (see page 101), in which the Shingle style tended to get the most emphasis. In these particular examples, the sense of a crossover between the Swiss Chalet and Craftsman styles was especially pronounced, for most of their interiors were decidedly Craftsman style in feeling, materials, and features.

Oriental Style

Although the term *Oriental* doesn't sound specific enough to connote an actual style, its generality seems particularly appropriate to describe most examples that displayed this influence, which, like the Swiss Chalet, was also among the earliest to be combined with the Craftsman style. One reason that a somewhat vague term makes sense is that it is not always clear exactly by which so-called Oriental influence a home's design may have been influenced. At the top of these mixed Oriental influences is Japanese design and architecture. Curiously, before the Craftsman style took on a stronger identity of its own, many of its early examples, particularly in southern California, were commonly perceived as a combined interpretation of both Swiss Chalet and Japanese architecture, linked by their extensive use of natural wood (SEE FIGURE 76). The woodsy character shared by many of Greene and Greene's early signature homes (including the Gamble house, Figure 66) was the reason their Pasadena neighborhood overlooking the Arroyo was nicknamed "Little Switzerland" for a time. Their specific style was actually dubbed "Japo-Swiss" before "Craftsman style" eventually displaced it.

Separate from that general impression that these two imported influences were somehow embodied in the Craftsman style, there are other parallels between the Swiss Chalet and Oriental styles. For example, developers felt that the novelty of the Oriental influence would also enhance a home's outward appeal and further promote its saleability, and it was used to invoke a more fanciful counterpoint in the relative sobriety of otherwise mostly Craftsman-style homes (SEE FIGURE 77). Similarly, it was also a popular early style influence that was used, sometimes flagrantly, to help sell many smaller bungalows. While less common, a number of larger-scale homes were subject to the same application of Oriental influence, although on some of these, its appearance was more limited and may have only shown up on some interior elements. In its most overtly blatant examples, the Oriental influence is certainly among the easiest of all to identify (SEE FIGURES 74 AND 75). In homes wrought with greater subtlety and sophistication, it tends to merge more quietly into the broader range of the Craftsman design vocabulary (SEE FIGURE 78).

By the early twentieth century, various degrees of Oriental influence had already been factors in examples of progressive architecture, interiors, and furnishings for much of the late nineteenth century. Although European trade with the Far East, especially China, had been active since long before the colonization of America, another important source of Oriental influence to consider is the mid-nineteenth-century resumption of world trade with Japan. Economically and culturally closed to the West for several centuries, Japan was at first widely perceived by the West as a culture where time stood still. In the decades following its initial reopening in the 1850s, Japanese exports fostered a bustling trade with Europe, and especially England, where the popularity and affordability of many typical goods eventually ignited a mania for all things Japanese. By the 1870s and 1880s especially, Japan was among other exotic cultures and their imports that were fodder for interpretation by proponents of the so-called Aesthetic movement that was at its most fashionable and influential both in England and America during that time.

In some ways a precursor to the later evolution of Arts and Crafts movement when greater simplicity ruled the roost, the Aesthetic movement was associated at the time to a certain degree with the early and more medieval-inspired phase of the

Figure 75.

HOUSE IN SANTA BARBARA, CALIFORNIA (CA. 1910).

Glimpsed through its embowered setting, another domestic rarity interprets the Oriental taste in an overtly literal manner. Although built on a larger scale, this home's right-hand portion has a pagoda-like form similar to the design in Figure 74. Consistent with Craftsman-style taste, its rafter tails are exposed under upswept eaves. Seen on these portions of the house are dramatic extensions of the structural (outrigger) beams of the roof ridges, which project from the ends of the sharply pointed gable peaks. Although its hillside landscape is now overgrown, the building was sited to take in the ocean views.

English Arts and Crafts movement. To some extent, it was admired if not embraced, by some of its proponents, such as William Morris and his circle; especially fascinating to them was the miraculous preservation of Japanese culture that its long isolation achieved. The remarkable beauty and vibrancy of newly imported Japanese goods, including silk fabrics, lacquerwork, woodblock prints, porcelains, and metalwork, began to indelibly redefine the standards of Western taste. The elegant simplicity of Japanese designs was certainly an inspiration that helped pave the way for the eventual emergence of the modern movement. The English Arts and Crafts movement viewed the time-honored artistic durability of Japanese designs as a parallel to England's own medieval craft traditions in their revival. In America, looking beyond the rampant superficiality that commonly colored much public perception of its significance, the Japanese influence would reach its apogee in the upcoming progressive work of Frank Lloyd Wright and other Prairie School adherents.

As definitive in its own exotic influence as the sheltering roof forms of Swiss Chalets, the roofs of Oriental-style homes reflect, in a fanciful way, something of the character of a pagoda. In those examples that adapted the pagoda's distinctively upswept eaves, the presence of exposed rafter tails beneath them is more obviously revealed (SEE FIGURES 74 AND 75). It is important to reiterate here that the visibility of such rafters, as well as other various framing members and structural elements that so typify the Craftsman style, owes a tremendous debt to traditional Japanese timber-frame construction. In evolution for many centuries and originally derived from ancient China, such traditional Japanese construction methods remain textbook examples of how the structural fabric of buildings becomes fully integrated into the overall impression of their design when it is allowed to remain outwardly apparent.

Figure 76.

HOUSE IN SOUTH PASADENA, CALIFORNIA (1907).

An otherwise predominantly Craftsman-style home is embellished here with Oriental-style influence. This large home was also deliberately designed to resemble a bungalow. While more abstracted than in the previous examples, slightly upturned gable ends still recall a pagoda-style roof. Offset to the left, two forward-facing gables are placed in alignment. As the house becomes higher toward the back, the repetition of these and the other gables helps reinforce a pagodalike effect. As with most of the other elements, large stylized brackets under the eaves appear more Craftsman than Oriental in style. Forms of traditional Japanese timber-frame construction are often cited as sources of the Craftsman style. Vertical siding on the porch gable's face, with cutout designs (for vents), suggests a reason why the nickname "Japo-Swiss" style was coined for such homes. The home's designer, G. Lawrence Stimson, was also the architect of the 1911 Wrigley mansion in Pasadena, now used as headquarters for the Tournament of Roses Association, the organization and namesake of the city's famous annual parade on New Year's Day.

Figure 77. (opposite)

HOUSE IN SAN DIEGO, CALIFORNIA (1917).

In the city's historic Burlingame district, this two-story house is a characteristic crossover example of a comfortable blending of the Craftsman and Oriental styles. It was built by Alexander Schreiber, who was responsible for the construction of numerous bungalow-era homes in this city. As in the previous example, most of the Oriental influence occurs in parts of its roof, which has gables with pagodalike peaks. In lieu of any brackets under the gables' eaves, a few large roof beams (purlins) project out into upwardly curving ends. Similar shapes occur above the massive porch columns. An influence of Chinese-derived fretwork is implied in the simple, irregular geometry of linear wood elements, displayed in silhouette, that appear in the open gable peak of the front porch. Craftsman-style statements are made by the square, stucco-faced porch columns, shingled walls, and windows.

Figure 78.

HOUSE IN DENVER, COLORADO (CA. 1915).

This substantial brick home's elusive style and unusual proportions and features suggest influences derived from both Craftsman and Oriental sources. Although its overall form is somewhat upstaged by the advancing features of its façade, the structure has a basic boxlike shape, overhanging hipped roof with exposed rafter tails, and central attic dormer; all common features of the American foursquare. Compared to the previous examples of Oriental-style influence, this makes a more abstract than literal statement. Supported on deep, highly stylized brackets, the double gable in front projects forward in the manner of an awning to shelter the balcony below. The paired peaks appear to break through the eaves of the hipped roof. Similarly detailed but at a smaller scale, the attic-level dormer is visible between them, and completes the grouping with its single, central peak. Intricate wood patterns used for the balcony railings recall the complex fretwork designs of Chinese-derived textiles and furniture forms. Exaggerated by the gables' deep eaves, Oriental influence is seen in the slightly upswept pagoda effect on either side of the double gable.

Figure 79. (opposite)

HOUSE IN LOS ANGELES, CALIFORNIA (1902).

With highly exaggerated peaks on its soaring roof gables and dormers, this house presents a truly eccentric example of Oriental influence. Sited on a corner in the historic West Adams district, it was built for Joseph Dupuy. Its unofficial local nickname, "The South Seas House," was prompted by its supposed resemblance to indigenous Polynesian dwellings with similarly shaped thatched-roof forms. It could also be said to recall the peaked roofs of Buddhist temples in Southeast Asia. The Craftsman style is apparent in the exposed rafter tails and in the river-rock facing used for the chimneys and porch-column piers. The diamond-pane windows, classically derived porch columns, and railing with turned spindles all evoke the Colonial Revival style. On the first floor at left is a modular configuration known as a "Chicago window," named for its association with use on that city's early skyscrapers. Allowing for maximum light and air circulation, the Chicago Window typically consists of a large fixed central panel flanked by two, usually double-hung, smaller windows. In this example, a fixed leaded-glass transom spans the entire assembly providing light and horizontal emphasis. Despite being a derelict eyesore for years, the building's picturesque form endeared it to the neighborhood, and local grassroots efforts finally saved it from certain destruction. Completely restored today, it has become a vibrant community center and a popular venue for neighborhood group meetings, activities, and special events.

CRAFTSMAN CROSSOVERS, PART II:
PROGRESSIVE AMERICANA

Prairie Style

WITH ITS ACTIVITY CENTERED IN America's upper Midwest, and with a particular focus in and around the Chicago area, a progressive movement in design and architecture was emerging by the end of the nineteenth century. Although what came to be called the Prairie style coincided closely with the arrival of the Arts and Crafts influence in America, the style truly may be considered an American original. Taking its name from French for "extensive meadow," the Prairie style of architecture was originally inspired by the ever-present sense of the horizon line that defines so much of the vast landscape of America's heartland. With good reason, people tend to associate the Prairie style with the work of architect Frank Lloyd Wright (1867–1959), but there is far more to its story than one man's influence. It was, in fact, a collective effort with contributions by many others, which made its eventual development possible.

In the years leading up to the Great Depression, the Prairie style was the most modern style ever seen in America, although the Craftsman style was considered by many, especially before World War I, to be almost as modern but less severe. The exteriors of Prairie-style homes offer a sharper contrast with the Craftsman style than most of the other crossover influences covered in this book.

Figure 80.

DESIGN FOR A HOUSE (1923).

This illustration was presented, with floor plans, in The Books of A Thousand Homes, a New York Home Owners Service Institute plan book. George W. Repp was credited as the architect. Although the term "Prairie style" was then not yet coined, the style had been in existence for over two decades and was America's most modern housing style. Described as "a type of architecture developed in the middle and western states," this home was "designed along horizontal lines," and "it fits into the landscape of the flat or rolling prairies." Characteristics include a low-pitched, hipped roof, with deep overhangs and squarely boxed-in eaves, and groupings of multiple casement-style windows. The divided windows and the patterned-brick insets pictured here were not typical of the early style. In plan, the central two-story section is a foursquare. Single-story extensions on each side linked by a line of eaves reinforce the symmetry. Wide horizontal clapboard siding below the first floor window sills grounds the design.

Figure 81.

HOUSE IN SAN DIEGO, CALIFORNIA (CA. 1915).

This Prairie-style home stands out among its Loma Portal neighbors, many of which reflect various historic revival styles of the later bungalow era. Obscured above the extended and fully enclosed eaves are hipped-roof forms with a very low pitch, appearing almost completely flat. Designed to fit on a fairly narrow urban lot, this house implies an effect of horizontality. A tall central chimney counterbalances an asymmetrical composition of separately readable parts, expressed in gradually ascending heights with separate roof levels. Unifying the design around the building's lower perimeter, a base is created by a horizontal line of molding that connects the first-floor windowsills. Substantial square porch posts further express the Prairie style. Used to highlight the groupings of casement windows, shallow projecting bays add further interest with their play of shadows.

Figure 82.

DR. T. ROBINSON BOURS HOUSE IN MILWAUKEE, WISCONSIN (1922).

Dr. Robinson and his wife Emma commissioned this Prairie-style house of Milwaukee architect Russell Barr Williamson, and it is considered his finest work. Williamson worked for Frank Lloyed Wright between 1914 and 1918, and was then the only employee entrusted to oversee construction of his projects. Built of buff-colored brick and trimmed in pale limestone, this house has overall massing similar to several Wright designs. Dominated by a rectangular two-story form, an enclosed single-story entry extends to the right. On an axis with the entry walk, the front door has an unusual semicircular glass transom that concentrically frames its rounded-arch top, outwardly expanding the door's proportions. A pair of attached columns (pilasters) flanks the living room's French doors, and support an overhanging structure with a built-in planter at its top. A large urn marks a front outdoor seating area that adjoins the living room beyond. The house was sited toward the inside property line of its corner lot. The current owner has landscaped the three sides of the house with Oriental-inspired gardens, providing the house with a sense of privacy.

Their interiors may offer more parallels, and in some examples, similarities. A strong sense of geometry usually is apparent in Prairie-style homes; the massing of their forms is most expressive of this. With considerable variances in scale, some may be interpreted as a self-contained, rectangular, box-like volume. Other examples with more room to spread out are often composed of a grouping of rectangular volumes; their arrangement may be anchored to the ground by a dominant one-story section, with a smaller two-story section carefully placed to form a sculptural composition. As its namesake implies, even in two-story examples horizontality echoes the prairie landscape. In fact, further reinforcement of this effect was often achieved with outdoor terraces extending outward from the house yet still linked to it by low, solid, railing-height walls of matching building materials. Echoing a design tenet of the Craftsman style, such devices allow the house to extend further into the landscape, and interact with it. It is not uncommon for strategically placed built-in planters, or pairs of low, stylized urns flanking walks or stairs, to be used to further reinforce Prairie designs.

Most often of hipped (pyramidal) form, Prairie roofs tend to have a rather shallow pitch, and at closer range, may appear to be completely flat (SEE FIGURES 80–82, 95 AND 101). Executed with boxy precision, their roof eaves extend outward with a deep cantilever, but their structural rafters are fully concealed from view, breaking with the Craftsman-style tenet of revealed construction. Placed together in smaller groupings or longer rows, windows break up the solid planes of the walls and reinforce the overall geometry of the house. The Prairie style is associated with a use of leaded art-glass windows, usually carried out in a thematic geometric design, often of highly stylized vegetation or other organic motifs (SEE FIGURES 85, 98, 99 AND 103), which might be repeated in various other places, such as interior built-in cabinetry, for further design consistency. A reflection of the area's harsher climate, most midwestern Prairie examples tend to be built of durable brick. Many favored the use of Roman brick, which presents a thinner, more linear profile to the bricks' repeating courses (SEE FIGURES 82 AND 101). When the Prairie style was expressed in other locations, it often tended to employ a painted stucco-wall finish instead (SEE FIGURE 81).

Development of The Chicago School

To clarify and better understand the Prairie style and its influence, some historic perspective is helpful. In the years leading up to its emergence and Wright's eventual prominence, the style had an illustrious incubation period; it is also an integral part of the collective work of a group of progressively minded architects that has been loosely referred to as being of the so-called "Chicago School" (not a specific reference to any institution). Much of the momentum that helped to generate its prominence was a result of the enormous building opportunities created in the wake of Chicago's disastrous fire of 1871. In the years that followed, Chicago became a magnet for ambitious architects, building engineers, and a host of other trade professionals who flocked there to take advantage of new opportunities. On Chicago itself, the impact of this was staggering, for its postfire boom fostered such rapid growth that it became the region's apex of business and industry, and soon burgeoned into a sprawling metropolis. As a result of this unprecedented boom, not just Chicago's, but also America's, architecture, as well as the creativity of its designers, came of age and became internationally acclaimed.

Most of the initial building activity after the Chicago fire was for the reconstruction of the city's devastated commercial heart. The ensuing building projects coincided with new developments in building design, technology, and engineering, and Chicago was at the epicenter. The best and brightest upcoming talents in the building industries came, and some would number among the most brilliant in our history. America's architectural training system was still evolving from a hands-on apprentice system to a formal course of study, and some of the younger generation were drawn to Chicago for potential on-the-job learning opportunities.

A major figure of influence in the Chicago school equation was Henry Hobson Richardson (1838–1886), one of America's greatest and most admired architects at the time, who was among the first from this country to study architecture at the prestigious Ecole des Beaux-Arts in Paris. Based in Boston, he worked on projects in Chicago, but by then he had already made his reputation nationally for his innovative design and planning in various public buildings. Among the most

famous of these remains Boston's 1876 Trinity Church. The high profile of his successes earned his signature style (Romanesque Revival), the soubriquet "Richardsonian Romanesque." Considered another masterpiece, his most lauded Chicago commission was the 1885 Marshall Field Wholesale Building (destroyed), which was widely influential both locally and nationally. However, an important residential project, Chicago's 1886 Glessner House, shows an influence of the English Arts and Crafts movement in its interiors, which include William Morris wallpapers. Remarkably intact, it is open to the public as a house museum.

From the next generation, a major figure among those of the Chicago School was a young architect named Louis Henri Sullivan (1856–1924), who went on to become the employer and acknowledged mentor of Frank Lloyd Wright. Greatly inspired by Richardson's work, Sullivan formed a fortuitous partnership with building engineer Dankmar Adler (Adler and Sullivan) in 1881; their commercial building projects famously pioneered advances in steel-frame construction, and gave birth to the American skyscraper. Alone in the midst of predominantly conventional Beaux Arts–inspired architecture, Sullivan's bold and original design for the Transportation Building at Chicago's World Columbian Exposition of 1893 stood out. In the mid-1890s Sullivan set out on his own, and produced some of his most

Figure 83.

PLEASANT HOME (JOHN FARSON HOUSE), OAK PARK, ILLINOIS (1897).

Architect George W. Maher's simplified sense of massing made this design a daringly progressive statement at the time. This imposing house presents itself as a broad, rectangular mass with a deep, full-width front porch, hipped roof, and central dormer. Pale Roman (thin-profile) brick walls detailed in limestone comprise the primary exterior finish materials. The signature motif is expressed in circular medallions on two front-porch columns as well as in the art-glass insets of the front door and its skylights, whose triple arches are shadowed at center within the porch. Lion-head masks of carved stone are mounted on the foundation wall, and originally disguised a pair of porch floor drain outlets. Restoration efforts should reinstate original details missing from the front façade, including an urn-topped second-floor balcony railing, and additional detailing around the top and sides of the dormer. To the left, the building extends further into its landscape with a single-story, semicircular side porch (now glass-enclosed, with rounded-arch windows), which opens to both the front porch and the living room. Glimpsed on the far right, a porte-cochère covers the side entrance and driveway.

Figure 84.

FRONT PORCH OF PLEASANT HOME.

Next to the sidewalk in front, part of the original iron fence (and one of its columns) surrounding the property is visible at center through the porch opening. Not an original Maher-designed feature but added later by the Mills family, the hand-made tile flooring design contributes a warm Arts and Crafts sensibility to the broad expanse. Anticipating their similar use inside, a series of incandescent electric lightbulbs outline the ceiling's perimeter, which lends a welcoming glow to the porch at night. Part of George Maher's original design, they reflect the architect's fascination with still-new lighting technology. In their early period of development, exposed lightbulbs were creatively handled by some architects, including Louis Sullivan, as glowing jewels, and often were used without shades, making a sparkling effect.

Figure 85. (opposite)

FRONT-ENTRY VESTIBULE OF PLEASANT HOME.

From the entry hall, the arching shape of the open doorway mirrors that of both inner and outer front doors (both out of view, to the right). Similar in design to those of their arch-topped sidelights (one is visible through the doorway), each door is fitted with a striking, leaded-art-glass panel. Also repeated on either side of the inner front door (one partly seen at left), the sidelights create a triple-arched ensemble that borrows daylight from its matching counterpart on the outside front wall. Like the art glass, the vestibule's mosaic tile floor interprets the floral and geometric motifs that George Maher chose for Pleasant Home. The hand-painted and stenciled decoration seen on the upper walls of these two areas was part of redecoration efforts undertaken by the Mills family (after 1910), during the earlier years of their occupancy. Visible at the upper left are a few of the original exposed electric lightbulbs used as an integral part of the entry hall's decorative scheme. The vestibule's mahogany woodwork contrasts with the quartersawn oak of the entry hall.

Figure 86. (opposite)

ENTRY HALL OF PLEASANT HOME.

At the heart of the house, this room makes a dazzling first impression with exposed electric light-bulbs highlighting the room's strong architectural elements of quartersawn oak. Opposite the front door is a low fireplace, faced in beautifully figured onyx, with a wood mantel on carved lion head corbels. "Pleasant Home" in gilded letters stretches across a wood panel above. At left, carved lion heads are on each side of a built-in bench upholstered in diamond-tufted velvet. Lined with downward-facing electric lights, a broad, flattened arch compresses the fireplace wall and its pair of recessed, arch-topped doors. Through a wide doorway to the dining room hung with portières (door draperies), an art-glass panel glows in a seating alcove. The painted wall decoration above the bench was a later addition by the Mills family after 1910.

inventive buildings, including Chicago's remarkable Carson, Pirie, Scott and Co. department store (1899–1904), originally built for Schlesinger and Meyer. While the advanced design of this project was widely acclaimed, it was due in part to difficult temperament and personal problems that Sullivan didn't achieve a comparable level of future success.

Believing that a unifying system of ornament was an appropriate complement to his buildings, Sullivan also likened his process of creating architecture to something organic. Some of his most celebrated work, such as the Carson, Pirie, Scott and Co. store, features distinctive detailing of literally organic forms of highly stylized vegetation, contemporary with and comparable to the sinuous motifs of the Art Nouveau style, another progressive design movement primarily centered in Europe. Along with other creative insights, Sullivan's organic building philosophy was earnestly adopted and would be taken further by his most famously gifted apprentice.

PLEASANT HOME (JOHN FARSON HOUSE),
OAK PARK, ILLINOIS (1897).

Important Chicago-area architect George Washington Maher (1864–1926) designed this early example of a Prairie-style home for John Farson (1855–1910), a wealthy banker, and his wife Mamie Ashworth Farson (1860–1941). Somewhat comparable to Louis Sullivan's design approach to an organic architecture, Maher pursued his own rhythm motif theory, in which he integrated thematic patterns and motifs, both inside and out, to give his projects a cohesive unity. Maher used this design approach for Pleasant Home, choosing the floral motif of an American honeysuckle combined with geometric circles and squares that occurs throughout the building. The spacious grounds that surround the house offset its massive scale. The Farsons were prominent Oak Park citizens, active in many local organizations and known for staging lavish parties. After John Farson's death in 1910, Mamie sold their house to Herbert Stephen Mills (1870–1929) and his wife, Leonie de Gignac Mills (1870–1930). The Mills fortune was made in the amusement machine business, which supplied a variety of mechanical attractions to popular penny arcade venues. Less socially engaged, this household of two adults and eight children was also less active in community affairs than the Farsons. In 1939, the house was purchased from the Mills family by the Park District of Oak Park, who renamed the grounds Mills Park and turned the house into a community center. Since 1969, the Historical Society of Oak Park and River Forest have used the upper floors to display their collections, and operate a local research center on the premises. Since 1990, the Pleasant Home Foundation, which is guiding the ongoing restoration of the structure, its interiors, and its grounds, has administrated the property. Today, the primary first-floor rooms of the house are open to the public as a house museum, and are available as a venue for special events.

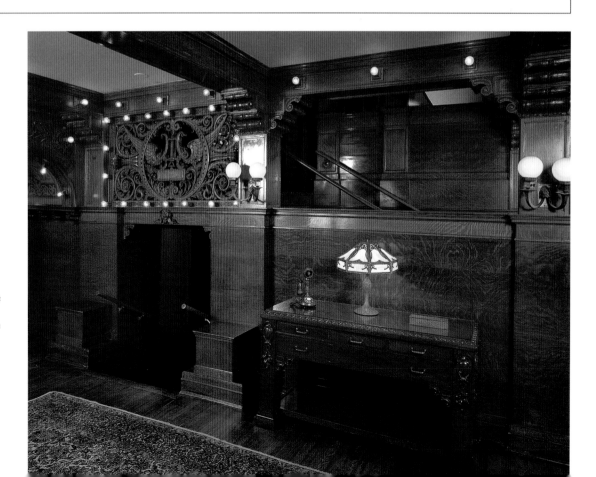

Figure 87.

DETAIL IN ENTRY HALL
OF PLEASANT HOME.

This area is to the right of the entry hall's fireplace. Designed to function as a large screen, this partly open wall shields the staircase (the handrails were added) as it rises from the base of the square column at right. Framed by electric lights, an intricately carved openwork panel surrounds a smaller panel incised with "music" beneath a winged lyre. This panel shields a sizable landing that opens into the music room through a wide doorway. During parties with live music, the portières in this doorway were opened, backlighting the panel with light and allowing the music to reach all of the public rooms. The side table with drawers is one of the original furniture pieces designed by George Maher that remain in Pleasant Home.

Figure 88.

DINING ROOM OF PLEASANT HOME.

*Planned for large-scale entertaining, this room and the adjoining living room have wide doorways (out of view at right) connecting
to the entry hall. The dining room retains much of the original furniture that Maher designed, including a dining table, a partial
set of chairs, a matching sideboard, a wall-mounted display cabinet, the ceiling fixture (once much lower), and the original
mirror on the fireplace mantel. A pair of art-glass windows in a seating alcove at left flank the door leading to a summer dining
room by the rear garden. Renovations removed the pocket doors between the living and dining rooms and widened the doorway.
When Pleasant Home was used as a community center, other "improvements" included recessed downlights and narrow ceiling
moldings, which are among later changes to be reversed in future restoration work.*

Frank Lloyd Wright and the Prairie School

Frank Lloyd Wright was to become the most noted of all the architects associated with the Prairie School. Before he started his own practice, he had already designed some houses before he left the firm of Adler and Sullivan, including his own home in Oak Park, Illinois, in 1889, with a later office and studio addition, all now open to the public as a house museum. Under the auspices of Adler and Sullivan, Wright participated in the design of the 1891 Charnley House in Chicago, which reveals much of his promise. His first commission on his own was the groundbreaking 1893 Winslow House in River Forest, Illinois. Beneath its boldly hovering hipped roof, the overall form of this house has a strong sense of horizontality, and largely fore-shadowed designs with similar features that would characterize Wright's later, more famous Prairie-style homes. In the Winslow House, Wright also employed a system of ornament, closely patterned after Sullivan's example, to articulate its otherwise simple form. His own interpretation of organic architecture was to evolve into a simpler, highly personalized style, but the profound influence of his master never ceased to affect his work.

In comparing the interiors of Wright's Prairie-style homes with some of the Craftsman style, parallels may be observed between them that suggest a shared Arts and Crafts influence. For example, the dominant horizontality that guides the proportions of the rooms and their woodwork detailing invites close comparison; furthermore, both focus on the centrality and importance of the fireplace. Another shared influence between the work of Wright and the Craftsman style is that of Japan. Less apparent in exteriors, the comparison of their interior planning is more apt. Many of Wright's plans are inspired by the multiple uses demanded of spaces in traditional Japanese homes, characterized by less-conventional, more flowing rooms that attempt to break out of the box (SEE FIGURES 102–6). In a manner that also evokes Japanese interiors, Wright liked to outline all four sides of interior walls in some of his Prairie-style homes with dark wood moldings to express each plane separately. It is interesting to note that for a number of years, Wright was also one of America's largest dealers of Japanese prints. He eventually worked in Japan, and the Imperial Hotel in Tokyo (1916–1922, destroyed) was one of his most celebrated commissions.

Before working there, Wright may have possibly gleaned some of his inspiration from exposure to the Japanese arts and traditional building techniques on display in an impressive exhibit at the 1893 World's Columbian Exposition, which included a perfect replica of an important timber-framed Japanese shrine. Coincidentally, on their way to Pasadena from

Figure 89.

LIBRARY OF PLEASANT HOME.

This recently restored room is reached through an arch-topped door to the right of the entry hall fireplace and also through a vestibule adjoining the kitchen. Forming one of the rear corners of the house, the curving wall at left is lined with large windows. The light green wall color and the green-glazed tile surround of the fireplace contrast well with the deep red mahogany woodwork. The arched mirror above the mantel is original, as are the incandescent lights mounted on a small perimeter cornice encircling the ceiling. The original domed ceiling fixture was reconstructed, but the long fringe is still missing. Repeating a motif from the entry hall, a carved-wood lion head appears on the built-in bookcases at right, and on additional bookcases to the far right that line an arch-topped alcove. Maher designed a round mahogany library table with the lion-head motif on its legs, but it has disappeared along with the other original furniture for this room.

Figure 90.

POWERS HOUSE, MINNEAPOLIS, MINNESOTA (1910).

Considered a landmark of progressive Prairie School architecture, this house was designed by Purcell, Feick, and Elmslie for businessman E. L. Powers, a vice president of the Butler Brothers mail merchandising company. Anchored by its brick-faced first floor, the house has a more vertical feeling than others of the Prairie style, but its horizontal elements are still strong. Bolstered by stone-capped brick buttresses around its base, the angled projection of the two-story bay window is the façade's most defining feature. In high contrast, the light color of the second-floor's stucco walls wraps uninterrupted onto the deep undersides of the fully enclosed eaves. The house's reverse plan innovatively positions the living room across the back, with views oriented onto the private garden and nearby Lake of the Isles. Across the front of the house, a screened porch (called Breakfast Porch on the original plans) adjoins the kitchen. A compact den with the angled bay window connects to the porch, and also opens to the dining room. The bay is placed on an axis with the living room's larger rounded bay window. The house and floor plans were featured in a 1913 issue of Western Architect.

the East Coast after completing their training, Charles and Henry Greene are also known to have visited the exposition, and the Japanese exhibit deeply impressed them. Although the brothers never traveled to Japan, its design traditions would soon become influential on their own architectural work in Pasadena, where they were destined to make their own history as the firm of Greene & Greene.

While Wright notoriously avoided giving credit to any influence other than his own genius, with the exception of his lifelong deference to Sullivan, some of his Prairie homes belie indebtedness to outside influences. For example, his work commonly incorporated many built-in features, such as benches and cabinetry, and favored cozy fireplace arrangements with adjacent built-in seating that seem clearly to be adaptations of the inglenook form, then a popular feature in so many Craftsman-style homes. Where Wright's Prairie-style homes clearly depart from the vast majority of Craftsman examples is that most of his were singular, custom-built projects, with fully integrated architecture, interiors, and furnishings, and his hand is visible in every detail. Wright's inspired designs for furniture and geometric art glass were widely admired.

Along with other peers similarly influenced by Sullivan, Wright became a charter member of the Chicago Arts and Crafts Society in 1897, which suggests that he was at least sympathetic to the tenets of the movement, and was willing to publicly support their validity. He would, however, remain somewhat removed from any sort of bandwagon thinking. Sometimes to the detriment of others, he was known for making scathingly opinionated pronouncements throughout his life.

In 1901, Wright made a compelling argument for the use of the machine in modern craft and building in a manifesto he presented called "The Art and Craft of the Machine." He argued that machines, if used correctly, could help achieve essentially the same idealistic goals of William Morris. Although Wright agreed with the Arts and Crafts tenet that using natural materials was noble and admirable, he was convinced that machines could be employed to achieve aesthetically inspired results. While controversial with more conservative Arts and Crafts devotees, this view foreshadowed the inspired goal of producing superior industrial designs for machine-manufactured goods, a cornerstone of progressive Modern movement teachings at the legendary Bauhaus school of design in pre-Nazi Germany, which flourished from the late 1910s through the 1920s.

Other Key Prairie School Contributors

During Wright's long career, despite the critical acclaim he received along the way, he remained consistently out of mainstream architecture as Sullivan had, but he remained a sympathetic teacher to younger aspirants of his profession. Among the most significant to pass through his employ was Walter Burley Griffin, who put his own stamp of originality on many innovative, Prairie-influenced home designs, particularly in a development at Mason City, Iowa. He later went on to mastermind the planning and architecture of the new capital city at Canberra, Australia. Griffin met his wife, Marion Mahoney, while both were working in Wright's Oak Park office. Also a draftsperson and designer, Mahoney was an especially gifted illustrator of architecture and interiors, and was responsible for rendering some of Wright's most impressive presentation drawings, for which he got much of the credit. Over the years, Wright pursued the idea of training young architects to his way of thinking, first in study programs he led at Taliesen, his Spring Green, Wisconsin, home and studio, and later at Taliesen West, in the Arizona desert, where his teaching legacy continues.

Other than Wright, Sullivan was also a formative influence on other architects who later achieved success on their own as part of the Prairie School. Among these

Figure 92.

LIVING ROOM OF THE POWERS HOUSE.

Enclosing a cushioned window seat, the living room's curving band of six casement windows pushes the house into the garden. On either side of its seats are low, built-in tables that frame the alcove. Centered on the wide doorway from the entry hall, the bay window commands the room. The current owners re-created Elmslie's design for the stenciled frieze with its subtle coloration and delicate patterning. Also characteristic of the architect's work are the crisply tailored, quartersawn oak moldings used to panelize the walls and ceiling. Other original, custom-designed features include the pair of wall sconces, and the geometric art-glass panels on French doors at the right, which open to the sunroom (now used as a music room). The same design motif is adapted on the glass doors of the room's bookcases (see Figure 94). With the sunroom on one end and a similarly sized inglenook on the other, the living room's strong lengthwise axis expands the spacious feeling. This room's views of Lake of the Isles have since been obscured by an added garage and mature vegetation.

Figure 91.

FRONT-DOOR SURROUND OF THE POWERS HOUSE.

Glazed a soft green with a matte finish, this robust example of Prairie School architectural terra-cotta ornament was designed by George Elmslie, the firm's acknowledged master of that genre. In the manner of previous work that he had produced for large commercial projects while under the employ of Louis Sullivan, Elmslie continued the use of ornament, and the organic architecture that Sullivan espoused. Highly stylized vegetation is coaxed and conventionalized into modular geometric units of ornament, where, in repetition over a larger area, their delicacy is transformed into a powerful effect. In the front door, a cutout motif (out of view at right) anticipates similarly stylized organic motifs used inside. The deep recess helps shelter the wooden door from the elements.

Figure 93.

DINING ROOM SIDEBOARD
OF THE POWERS HOUSE.

The attenuated lines of the sideboard have a spare, elegant quality. Although slightly recessed into its own alcove and neatly tied into the room's baseboard, it resembles a piece of freestanding furniture. Placed on an inside wall that abuts the kitchen, (reached through the door to the left), its sculptural quality is in harmony with the other design details in this house and incorporates some of the same geometric motifs. Otherwise quite spare, the piece has shallow carving on its pair of cupboard doors, and fully cutout panels on its slab-like sides, which are similar in form to a larger version used on the front door. Visible in period photographs of the room, built-in light fixtures were originally mounted on each of the upper front corners of the sideboard. The stenciled frieze re-creates another one of the home's original designs by Elmslie.

Figure 94.

LIVING ROOM INGLENOOK OF THE POWERS HOUSE.

To the left of the bay window, this inglenook holds a Prairie School treasure. The polychromatic, glazed terra-cotta ornament on the face of fireplace is a testament to the decorative genius of George Elmslie. He brilliantly adapted the organic forms of coiling vines and berries into a bold abstraction. Proving too costly, this is the only such example in the architect's residential interiors, but as an architectural finish material, it was a key component of many large commercial projects across the country, including skyscrapers. Used mostly for exterior cladding, its use persisted well into the 1930s. Viewed through a simplified colonnade, the fireplace treatment is enhanced by the framework of its inglenook setting, which contains an outside window to the right. The low, wide proportions of the fireplace opening and raised hearth anticipate modern examples. Built-in storage cabinets between the rectangular posts and the walls face the fireplace. Turned sideways, the motif on the art-glass panels of the bookcase doors at left s similar to the one on the sunroom's French doors (see Figure 92).

was George Grant Elmslie (1869–1952), an immigrant from Scotland, who first secured, with Wright's help, a job in Sullivan's office in 1895. Elmslie worked diligently for the next fourteen years as Sullivan's chief draftsman, and was closely involved with some of his most important projects. Like Wright, he became a devout disciple of Sullivan's philosophy of organic architecture; he also had a particular gift for interpreting the master's signature vocabulary of highly stylized, vegetation-inspired ornament (SEE FIGURES 91 AND 94). His own artistic brilliance is often overlooked.

In 1903, impressed by the aspirations of a progressive young architect named William Gray Purcell (1880–1965), Elmslie hired him to work in Sullivan's office; although employed there only briefly, Purcell was deeply inspired by the experience. In 1906, after taking other work on the West Coast for a couple of years, Purcell and former Cornell classmate George Feick Jr. (1881–1945) made a revelatory visit to Europe, observing its latest architectural trends, and decided to open their own office upon their return. Setting up a practice in Minneapolis, Minnesota, a then-booming city, they attracted a clientele who welcomed their forward-thinking home designs that interpreted and expressed organic architecture. In 1910, after leaving Louis Sullivan's by then financially strapped office, George Elmslie was invited by Purcell and Feick to join their growing firm, and they all worked together until Feick left in 1913. Their work was showcased in the *Western Architect* as among the best new designs of the day in both 1913 and 1915. While long-term success eluded them, the firm of Purcell and Elmslie continued in practice before its final dissolution in 1921. Among their most innovative and acclaimed Minneapolis commissions are the 1910 E. L. Powers House (FIGURES 90–94), and the 1913 Purcell-Cutts House

(FIGURES 95–100). In recent years, the talents and importance of this firm have become more widely recognized and heralded.

Another significant architect who emerged from the Chicago School was George Washington Maher (1864–1926), who came to Chicago in the early 1880s and first worked as a draftsman for the firm of Bauer and Hill. In 1887, he secured a job in the office of Joseph Lymnan Silsbee, then a fashionable architect of homes for a nouveau riche clientele. Silsbee had quite a knack for recognizing young talent, for there, Maher found himself working alongside George Grant Elmslie and Frank Lloyd Wright. In 1888, Maher opened his own practice, at first working in then-popular historic revival styles, but soon evolving in more progressive directions. As a prolific writer, he found an outlet for his opinions, addressing the need for a new American architecture as early as 1889. An early expression of Prairie School tenets, his design for the 1897 Pleasant Home (or the John Farson House) in Oak Park, Illinois (FIGURES 83–89), remains a superb example of his formidable talents, which deserve more recognition.

The specific term *Prairie School* was actually coined by Wright as an observation in retrospect. He first used it in 1936, as a way of referencing the specific category of his own work built after 1893, but completed before 1910. Since then, historians who describe the architecture and design of that period have sanctioned those general dates and the Prairie School label to that period. The term applies to specific works by various architects who were clearly inspired by Louis Sullivan. The term *Prairie School* is also used to help separate the work of its architects from that of Sullivan himself. The contributions of these generations of progressive architects from the upper Midwest comprise some of America's finest and most original examples of proto-modern design.

PURCELL-CUTTS (EDNA S. PURCELL) HOUSE, MINNEAPOLIS, MINNESOTA (1913).

One of the most important projects designed by the firm of Purcell, Feick, and Elmslie was the residence for firm partner William Purcell and his family. During the planning process, the firm assigned the wife's name to the project, for its original drawings are titled "Edna S. Purcell Dwelling." All involved agreed this was an opportunity for the firm's collective progressive design talents to be showcased. Because the Purcells were active in various arts and social groups and since Edna was also a skilled musician, they needed a suitable place to entertain, as well as to raise their young family. Purcell later concluded that this project was "perhaps the most complete dwelling" of all his later collaborations with Elmslie (Feick left the firm the year this house was built). With his father's financial aid, Purcell's home cost about $14,000, then considerably more expensive than other 3,200-square-foot homes. As the firm's new commissions eventually declined, the Purcells decided to seek work elsewhere and sold their dream home to Anson B. Cutts, Sr. in 1919. In 1985, his son, Anson B. Cutts Jr., bequeathed the house to the Minneapolis Society of Fine Arts. He also left some of his family's furnishings, as well as funds for the restoration of the house. The Minneapolis Institute of Arts was assigned by its parent organization the responsibility to completely restore and refurnish the house. In 1990, the Purcell-Cutts House opened to the public as a house museum.

Figure 95.

PURCELL-CUTTS (EDNA S. PURCELL) HOUSE,
MINNEAPOLIS, MINNESOTA (1913).

This home stands out as strikingly modern in a neighborhood of mostly Historic Revival-style homes. The house is sited further back than its neighbors, allowing for a generous front garden and reflecting pool, a partial view of nearby Lake of the Isles from the back, and views from the dining room of neighboring gardens. Counterbalanced by a tall chimney, the compact horizontal design unfolds as an asymmetrical composition of rectangular volumes with shallowly pitched hipped-roof forms, and deeply cantilevered, enclosed eaves. Leaded art glass with geometric Prairie style designs is used extensively throughout. The front door is offset and recessed under a small covered porch at right. The warm stucco walls harmonize with the exposed trim elements of darkened cypress. A geometric stenciled frieze was applied around the top of the house.

Figure 96.

FRONT DOOR OF THE PURCELL-CUTTS HOUSE.

The original art glass in the front door and sidelights employs the distinctive geometric motifs repeated throughout the house. In a whimsical touch, stylized lettering spells out the words "Peek-a-Boo" at the top of each sidelight. The playfully positioned words at left face outside, while those on the right are turned inward. Humor seems to have been a prevailing factor around this house, for George Elmslie also nicknamed this project the "Little Joker." Characteristic waxed-oak woodwork details complement the warm, sandy wall color in the public spaces. Unlike most other homes of that time, the Purcells felt that an open, informal floor plan should be a crucial aspect of their progressive design. This entry hall space is a large, open landing which serves as the pivotal circulation point of the split-level home. The living and dining rooms are to the right, with service areas and a side entrance toward the left.

Figure 97.

LIVING ROOM (TOWARD THE FRONT) OF THE PURCELL-CUTTS HOUSE.

The room's finishes and furnishings have been restored to the time of the Purcells' original occupancy. Fronted by a raised hearth, the low, wide fireplace opening and its broad surround are of Roman (thin-profile) brick favored by Prairie School architects. Iridescent glass is embedded between the bricks in the mortar. A thick lintel of purplish Minnesota sandstone sits flush to both bricks and wall. With the woodwork elements already in place, illustrator Charles Livingston Bull painted a mural of Louisiana herons in flight against a moonlit sky and moss-draped trees. Elmslie added more refined wood to enhance the mural, as well as pendant lights and bands of stencil decoration. The dramatic wall of art glass windows facing the street is underscored by a full-width window seat. The pair of chairs and tall pedestal replicate original Elmslie-designed pieces. The steps at far left lead to the front entry. The stenciled borders around the perimeter areas of the "tent" ceiling (so named because of it peaked, tent-like shape) continue into the adjacent dining room.

Figure 98. (opposite)

LIVING ROOM (TOWARD THE BACK)
OF THE PURCELL-CUTTS HOUSE.

A distinctive partial-height wall, dominated by a pointed form resembling a ship's prow, divides the different levels of the open living and dining rooms, which share a tent ceiling. The prow's leaded-art-glass doors containing built-in storage cabinets repeat the established thematic designs. The right cabinet door hides its true function as a cold-air return. Beneath the prow's peak, the baseboard and wall were undercut to allow the area carpet to slide beneath. Designed as a sculpture pedestal, the prow supports a Richard Bock patinated plaster figure of Nils, a Swedish children's book hero, astride a flying goose. The art-glass bookcase doors of the cozy writing nook match those of the prow. The chair with the triangulated back is an Elmslie design. At far left, a dictionary stand with an art-glass inset replicates another Elmslie-designed piece.

Figure 99.

DINING ROOM OF THE PURCELL-CUTTS HOUSE.

Since the floor level here is significantly higher than in the living room, the dining room has a lower, more intimate feeling. Tall built-in lighting fixtures flank an alcove with a corner grouping of distinctive art glass windows, whose design is repeated in the rear French doors. An adjoining screened porch on the back is partly visible through the doors. When this house was to be featured in a 1915 issue of the Western Architect, the Purcells borrowed a set of Elmslie-designed dining furniture for the photographs. The dining furniture here today is a reproduction of the same mahogany set borrowed for the period photographs. The triangulated chair backs are embellished with art-glass inlays, and the table features linear inlaid lines on its top and square motifs on its legs.

Figure 100.

MASTER BEDROOM SUITE OF THE PURCELL-CUTTS HOUSE.

The second-floor level of the house was designed for efficient use of space, but its approach maintains the airy feeling of the lower levels. Lit by art-glass windows on three sides of its mid-floor landing, the spacious stair hall has its own tent ceiling, encircled by Elmslie-designed stenciling. Seen through two doorways, the master bedroom suite was designed to be separately accessed rooms. Suspended from a ceiling track and secured to the floor, a folding grass-cloth-covered partition created a movable wall. The room's left portion was initially planned as an east-facing morning room for the right-side, larger bedroom, which has a roomy corner closet and adjoins a sleeping porch. In 1915, inspired by Pullman-style train beds, Purcell designed the small built-in bed at left for his four-year-old son, James. The Purcells adopted their second child, Douglas, that same year. With the Pullman bed's built-in drawers and cupboards below, little other bedroom furniture was required. Another of Elmslie's stenciled border designs appears in both of these areas.

Figure 101.

BOGK HOUSE, MILWAUKEE, WISCONSIN (1916).

Designed by Frank Lloyd Wright, this elegant urban house was built for Frederick C. Bogk, a Milwaukee businessman and politician, and is among the finest works of Wright's later Prairie period. It has been occupied by its current owners since 1955. Some exterior detailing anticipates Wright's forays into other styles and influences; a geometric frieze of cast concrete above the front windows includes parts that resemble abstracted Mayan figures. Deep eaves project five and a half feet, obscuring the home's hipped roof at close range. A low wall flanked by urns encloses a private front patio adjoining the living room. The windows are recessed into slitlike channels that provide vertical elements in the mostly horizontal design. The house cost $15,000 to build. Since Wright was working in California and Japan at the time, Russell Barr Williamson (see Figure 82) supervised its construction.

Figure 103.

LIVING ROOM (TOWARD THE FRONT) OF THE BOGK HOUSE.

Three sets of velvet-draped French doors open to the walled front patio area. Pairs of narrow, geometric-design, art glass sidelights flank each set of doors, and larger panels of similar design are on the wall. Metallic gold and silver paint are part of the original scheme. George Niedecken modified the desklike library table from a Wright design. Its motif of small repeating squares is characteristic of early-twentieth-century European Secessionist decorative arts. After receiving an inquiry about design advice for their home shortly after acquiring it, Wright referred the current owners to Henredon, then production manufacturers of a line of recent Wright-designed furniture. The side chair at the library table is from that collection. Wright-trained architects from Taliesen West in Arizona helped remodel the outdated kitchen and added the square recessed downlights around the living room. The Taliesen studio also designed several new furniture pieces for the house, including a pair of armchairs with footstools (seen at left), and some taller stools with tasseled seat cushions (seen in Figures 102 and 104).

Figure 102.

LIVING ROOM (TOWARD THE SIDE) OF THE BOGK HOUSE.

Wright collaborated on this project with important Milwaukee interior designer George Mann Niedecken (1878-1945). Niedecken's significant contributions to Wright projects have often been misattributed or overlooked during the ensuing years. An open, flowing feeling pervades the Bogk House interiors. Walnut woodwork is used throughout the first floor, while gumwood appears in the upstairs rooms. In the foreground, part of a low wall, with inlaid ebonized squares on the edges of built-in cabinetry, adjoins the central fireplace. The carefully placed geometric forms in studied directional groupings on the room's area carpet reproduce Wright's original design. In the 1960s, when the old carpet was rewoven in the same design for the current owners, Wright's widow, Olgivanna, revised its color scheme with more vivid hues. Note the Niedecken design of the window valances, which feature cutout wood motifs against a gold leaf ground. These adapt the form of Japanese rammas (wooden transom screens). The front door is behind the partial-height wall with bookcases and a recessed art-glass fixture.

Figure 104.

LIVING ROOM FIREPLACE OF THE BOGK HOUSE.

The central importance of the fireplace, both symbolic and practical, is a constant in Wright's domestic designs. Built-ins with bookcases around the fireplace create a low wall that divides the living room from the front entry. Facing the fireplace is a cushioned bench seat, creating an inglenook effect, and (to the left), a side table with drawers. The front door is located behind this built-in feature, which is lined by bookshelves on its opposite side. In the foreground, the pair of armless lounge chairs, side chair, and small occasional tables are among the 1950s pieces from Hendredon's Wright-designed collection. Dark mortar between the narrow brick joints and light mortar between each course of bricks creates the clean-lined effect of horizontal stripes, which is a continuation of the exterior masonry treatment. A mosaic tile hearth extends from the fireplace, and reflecting firelight reveals the tile pattern.

Figure 105.

GARDEN ALCOVE OF THE BOGK HOUSE.

A window-lined alcove projects outward from the dining room, and overlooks an outside built-in planter. A glass door resembling a window on the left side of the alcove opens to the rear garden. Both the metallic silver frieze and ceiling moldings are continued into the alcove. Anchoring the steps, the built-in brick planter incorporates wooden lanterns, attached to square posts rising to the underside of the crossing shelf above. A geometric banding of cut stone around the top of the planter repeats on the lower right brick wall behind the fountain. Water flows from a slot in a low-relief stone panel of stylized storks into a small rectangular basin. A delicately scaled pattern of mosaic tile adorns the dining room and garden alcove floors, in contrast with the living room's oak flooring.

Figure 106.

DINING ROOM OF THE BOGK HOUSE.

Raised above the living room but sharing the same ceiling plane, the dining room repeats many design motifs of the living room such as the square, recessed downlights and the narrow, geometric, art-glass sidelights. Set flush to the wall, a built-in sideboard creates a display niche with narrow, art-glass wall lights, and horizontal bands of walnut molding. The dining furniture is original, the current owners having acquired it from a Bogk daughter. The same edging of inlaid squares seen on the living room pieces repeats on the tables, server, and built-in sideboard. At the request of Mrs. Bogk, George Niedecken revised some of Wright's designs. Among his changes were to use caned chair backs instead of Wright's square spindles and to span the table legs with caned panels. He also designed the room's Oriental lantern-style central fixture, and a pendant-style fixture at far right, which hangs near an original card table and chairs in that corner.

Shingle Style

Although as uniquely American as the Prairie style, the Shingle style has more specific links to our historic past, and evolved over a longer period. Unrelated to any Arts and Crafts influence at first, it was inspired by some surviving and mostly utilitarian buildings dating to our Colonial period—simple vernacular structures, distinguished chiefly by the unifying texture of plain wooden shingles that covered their walls and roofs. Becoming associated with progressive architecture from an early date, the Shingle style may also be considered as a related aspect of the Colonial Revival movement, which got underway after America's 1876 Centennial celebration instilled new pride in our history and a stronger sense of nationalism. The first phase of the Shingle style occurred mostly in the 1880s and 1890s. The durability and attractive weathering qualities of shingled walls encouraged its emergence as a fashionable style for the summer homes of many wealthy East Coast families. At first it was most likely to be found in seaside locations of New England, where so much evidence of our Colonial past is still present.

Eventually, the Shingle style would manifest itself as an influence on Craftsman-style homes. Identified easily, the Shingle style's most obvious and significant statement is made through the use of shingled walls. There is an appealing simplicity and practical certainty about this simple surface that conveniently dovetailed with Arts and Crafts aesthetics. Enlivened by a play of light and shadow across it throughout the day, a shingled surface derives most of its interest from its distinctive texture. However,

unlike the typical Craftsman-style building's deep roof overhangs, most true Shingle-style buildings have very shallow, if any, roof overhangs, which serves to unite the overall form of the house with that of the roof. This is one of the reasons the style appealed to progressive architects, for they found great creative freedom in composing a building's exterior spatial volumes without as much of the usual hierarchy of walls versus roof. In the most successful Shingle-style designs, these two are blended into a single, unified composition, bridged by the commonality of all their outer surfaces. This sculptural quality is often entirely absent from Craftsman-style homes, including many bungalows, which tended to employ shingled walls mainly for their added textural interest. In many Craftsman variations, horizontal clapboard siding may be used to express the first floor, while the second floor may feature contrasting shingles.

In many Shingle-style examples, a minimal emphasis is given to the outer frames (or casings) of window and door openings, which are allowed to simply recede into their textured backgrounds (SEE FIGURES 107–111). Another typical Shingle-style detail is the use of shallow, outwardly flared overhangs between floor levels, or above some door and window openings; these provide shelter, but are primarily used as a device that further exploits the play of light and shadow across the shingled wall surface. Sometimes the successive courses, or rows, of shingles were applied in alternating widths, creating further interest with a banded pattern. In

Figure 108. (opposite)

HOUSE IN ROCHESTER, NEW YORK (CA. 1910).

The swooping "catslide" roof that covers the front porch of this house is a feature that might appear on either Shingle or Craftsman style homes. Typical of the Shingle style, shallow eaves appear on the gable of the front dormer, whose slightly kicked-up eaves echo the movement of the front catslide. Opening to a shallow balcony set into the roof's slope, a former sleeping porch is enclosed in the dormer. While the side gable's eaves are slightly deeper, their lack of exposed structural elements suggest a Colonial Revival or Shingle rather than Craftsman-style influence. On the side, around the top of the recessed attic-level window, the shingle courses are laid in concentric rings and repeat the shape of its rounded top. The railing of this recess is detailed like a miniature balcony, and appeared on similar late-Queen Anne or early-Shingle-style homes. Stone in the first-floor walls and square porch columns are compatible with either the Shingle and Craftsman styles.

Figure 107.

DESIGN FOR A HOUSE (1900).

This plan book design , seen in Shoppell's Modern Houses, has the prominent roof and ground-hugging quality of bungalows in the emerging Craftsman style. Low, stone walls as well as stone front porch columns, and the porte cochère, also follow that style. Yet the shallow eaves of the overhanging, shingle-covered second story and the style of its roof and gables are Shingle-style characteristics. The preponderance of shingled surfaces on the roofs and walls unified such houses, and gave their forms a sculptural potential. On the left side, the oval accent window, the bowfront dormer, and the multipaned window sash are Colonial Revival details. The tall, narrow attic vent with an arched top is primarily a Shingle-style detail. Based on New York's going rates in 1900, the home's estimated cost was $4,500.

Figure 109.

HOUSE IN LOS ANGELES, CALIFORNIA (1906).

Designed by noted local architect Arthur B. Benton, this quirky yet sophisticated Shingle-style hybrid is in the historic Angelino Heights district. The square columns, exposed rafter tails, and double-gabled dormer with deep eaves are Craftsman-style details. Shingle courses outlining the arch in the end gable peak above the porch and the minimal use of trim on the second story are typical of the Shingle style. The rhythmic flattened arches, which seem to spring from the porch posts, imply the Colonial Revival. In the large upper front gable, two groupings of three narrow arched windows are stepped in height to align with the roof, echoing forms of the Mission Revival style. The front gables' eaves are punctuated by the ends of projecting roof beams (purlins). Set into the porch roof, the solid railing of a deck runs along the left side.

THE FIRST BAY TRADITION

Since the opening of the transcontinental railway system, there were vast changes in the public perception of our western frontier. Its new accessibility spiked rapid growth, particularly on the West Coast, which offered many of the same kinds of new opportunities for architects as Chicago had in the 1870s. At the center of most new development in California was San Francisco and the surrounding Bay Area, which had first boomed significantly in the years following the Gold Rush of 1849. By the 1890s, San Francisco had matured into a sophisticated metropolis, a center of money and power that attracted a wave of new architects. Many of these were from the East Coast, and most were conversant in whatever trends were afoot in the building industry. Many of these architects were also of the younger generation, and could also boast of far better educations than most others who had preceded them to the Bay Area. It was into this climate that the area's first phase of the progressive architecture, now called the "First Bay Tradition," was born in the 1890s. The primary vehicle of its earliest examples was the East Coast—imported Shingle style. In a different way than it had in the Colonial Revival context of the East Coast, the humble quality of this material seemed to resonate in the California landscape as a natural companion. Furthermore, the early Shingle-style buildings of the West Coast also show how its development was carried to a new level of creativity. After 1900, its evolution continued, but by then it was becoming more associated as an influence, along with that of the Swiss Chalet, on the newly emerging Craftsman style that would be so vigorously expressed in the West. Perhaps the most famous and imaginative progressive architect of the First Bay Tradition to explore and exploit new territory in the context of the Shingle style was Bernard Maybeck (1862–1937) (SEE FIGURES 110–12), but other Bay Area architects also made brilliant contributions in the same vein, including A. Page Brown, Ernest Coxhead, John Galen Howard, Julia Morgan, Louis C. Mullgardt, Willis Polk, and A. C. Schweinfurth.

Figure 110.

END VIEW OF THE CHICK HOUSE, OAKLAND, CALIFORNIA (1913).

A remarkable example of progressive early-twentieth-century Bay Area architecture, this house designed by Bernard Maybeck is one of his most masterful domestic projects. By this date, Maybeck was known for his unusual and creative Shingle, Craftsman and Swiss Chalet inspired dwellings, with their seamless blending into the hilly local landscape. These influences are detected in this design. Sited in a canyon area studded with mature oaks, the Chick House was planned to embrace nature. While predominantly shingled, vertical board-and-batten siding sheathes its projecting gable ends. The upstairs corners project diagonally like medieval turrets and contain bedroom closets. With their exposed structure of open trelliswork, the deep eaves of the gable peak display a graphic pattern of layered timbers. Made of plain cast concrete but elegantly proportioned, the chimney of the living room fireplace incorporates more trelliswork. The display pedestal for a vase is another unexpected detail. The living room occupies this end of the first floor (see Figure 112).

some other early examples, shingled courses were placed to rise and fall in a gentle curve as they passed over the top of door and window openings. In a "ripple effect," it would be transmitted to several successive courses of shingles, animating the overall even texture of the wall with dynamic movement (SEE FIGURES 109 AND 111).

The overall form of many Shingle-style homes may betray a Colonial Revival link, for the gambrel roof, an ingredient of so-called Dutch Colonial–style homes, was especially popular with this style (SEE FIGURE 114). This common crossover influence is also seen in the use of Colonial Revival–inspired detailing on otherwise Shingle-style homes, such as classical columns, and diamond-paned windows. The same influence was known to routinely cross over into Craftsman-style homes as well. The American foursquare, especially in its earlier examples, was also subject to applications of the Shingle style (SEE FIGURE 23).

Despite its historic sources, the Shingle style was still considered a new style, one that didn't overtly flaunt the past, which set it apart from almost every other nineteenth-century style that had come before. One of the most appealing qualities that made it popular (especially for summer homes) was its heightened sense of informality, which most people greeted with enthusiasm. At a time when typical Victorian-era house plans were rather rigidly compartmentalized in accord with widely accepted social and family standards then in place, the Shingle style's more relaxed planning offered a breath of fresh air. In this sense, it recalled the similar appeal of many Rustic-style homes, and each foreshadowed qualities of the Craftsman style that had yet to develop.

Most famously, the Shingle style entered the repertoire of one of America's most important architectural firms, McKim, Mead and White, whose rambling Shingle-style domestic designs are considered some of the best examples of its early phase. In fact, one member of that firm had a direct link to launching more widespread interest in the style before few others had ever considered it. Charles Follen McKim (1847–1909) was then closely involved in an 1874 periodical called the *New York Sketch Book of Architecture*, and he undertook a study of existing Colonial-era buildings, accompanying it with newly commissioned photography. Examples were documented in their then-current condition, which was rather dilapidated in some cases. Some images appeared in the periodical, while a separate portfolio of all of them was published and distributed privately. One of the examples, the Bishop Berkeley House (circa 1729), in Middletown, Rhode Island, resonated most with McKim. In a photo of the rear view of this house, its slightly irregular shingled structure is largely defined by the long slope of a somewhat sagging shingled roof, in the manner of a so-called saltbox form. McKim's interest in such buildings, along with the photographs he assembled, helped jump-start both the Shingle style and the earliest traces of the coming Colonial Revival.

In light of his reassessment of this and other buildings he helped document, Charles McKim's revelation was that even the most outwardly humble structures were important examples of American heritage and as noble in their own right and as deserving of emulation as the fancier, more sophisticated building designs more often associated with the Colonial era. His sentiments galvanized his firm's inspiration to pursue interpretations of these simple, shingled structures, to be used as models for a new kind of artistic home for their very wealthy clients. It would take a while before

Figure 111.

REAR VIEW OF THE CHICK HOUSE.

Dominated by refined Shingle-style detailing, this side of the house also has Craftsman-style elements, as well as rather playful accents of Gothic and Classical styles. Above the concrete foundation line, the shingles are diagonally cut to create a cross-hatched pattern, which borders the outwardly flaring skirts of the lower walls, and also repeats above the door and window openings of the first floor. At left, a flattened Tudor arch outlines a recessed service entrance. A low railing, lined with turned balusters in the Classical mode, marks the exterior basement stairs. The railing's Prussian blue accent, as well as the red highlighting of the rafter tails, gate and balcony railing, reflect Maybeck's original color scheme. Improbably large brackets support a shed roof over a second floor balcony, which shelters the primary rear entrance. Sheltered by a smaller shed roof at right is a built-in concrete bench that is integrated with the foundation. A retaining wall abuts the raised rear garden area.

Figure 112. (opposite)

LIVING ROOM OF THE CHICK HOUSE.

The restrained design of the fireplace, with its unusually high and wide opening, is executed in cast concrete, which Maybeck liked to use in unconventional ways. Two raised platforms flanking the fireplace opening can be used as occasional seating. Framed by cast facsimiles of classical molding, the face of the fireplace features a recessed panel above the opening, in lieu of any mantel shelf. Towering pilasters on either side rise to the ceiling beams which align with the fireplace. Original to Maybeck's design, these beams are fitted with indirect cove lighting. Appropriately scaled for this space, the oversized French doors allow for plentiful daylight and generous views of the splendid natural setting, and occur on three sides of the room. An inlaid vintage English Arts and Crafts armchair is at left.

Figure 113.

SHOGREN HOUSE, PORTLAND, OREGON (1906).

Combining both Shingle and Craftsman styles, this home sits in the midst of a hilltop garden and is accessible to the public for special events. Fred A. Shogren commissioned this home from Portland architect Josef Jacobberger. A large forward-facing dormer (at right) caps a two-and-a-half-story rectangular box with side-gabled roof. A generous recessed porch features massive tapering stone columns supporting projecting beams with details in the manner of a pergola. A rounded, two-story tower is anchored by an oversized, rustic stonework chimney. Inside the tower is an inglenook that opens to the living room. In the upper gable, diamond-paned windows are arranged in a stepped formation paralleling the roof slope. Deep overhangs of simply detailed eaves show off the exposed rafter tails. The house is secluded within large, parklike grounds.

Figure 114. (opposite)

HOUSE IN LOS ANGELES, CALIFORNIA (1903).

Boldly proportioned, this house is reminiscent of rambling, northeastern, Shingle-style vacation homes and was built for William Gilbert. Partially concealed by the Queen Anne–style tower, an enormous forward-facing gable presides over the façade. On the left, a condensed version of the same form faces to the side. In typical Shingle style, each gable top projects to shelter attic-level windows. The eaves are fully enclosed behind angled shingling. Although the upper roof areas, including the conical part, are clad in green composition shingles, the lower side of the gable at left is wood-shingled, blending right into the wall of the adjoining tower. Cast concrete resembling masonry blocks with alternating textures defines the first-floor walls, the porch columns, the decorative panels above window openings, and the areas flanking the front stairs.

Figure 115.

FLETCHER HOUSE, WINNETKA, ILLINOIS (1901, WITH LATER ADDITIONS).

A few simplified Craftsman details, such as the prominent angled brace to the left of the front gable, and the dominant texture of shingled surfaces on both its walls and roof, impart interest to this home's exterior. The main part of the original house features a prominent gable, although overhanging eaves and a projecting upper face make it appear lower. Across the front, a row of towering windows lights the living room (see Figure 116). On the left side is a window-lined bay (partly seen) that encloses a dining alcove open to the living room (see Figure 117). Additions made in 1906 include a screened front porch, a shed-style dormer and a two-story section of bedroom space, all sensitively done with the styles and detailing matching the original. The same approach was taken in the recent addition of a family room on the far right side.

FLETCHER HOUSE, WINNETKA, ILLINOIS (1901).

First designed by architect Augustus B. Higginson for a young bachelor named Edwin S. Fletcher, this intriguing house retains much of the modest shingled demeanor and low-slung posture of its beginnings. Higginson was schooled at Harvard and studied in Europe before opening his Chicago practice in 1895. He and his wife, Frances, were an artistic couple drawn to the Arts and Crafts aesthetic. They built their own home in Winnetka, and furnished it with pieces of their own handiwork. In 1897, they were among the charter members of the Chicago Arts and Crafts Society, which also included Frank Lloyd Wright. It was during this time that they became acquainted with Edwin Fletcher, who became their client. Then an enclave of artistic and literary people, Winnetka was where Fletcher had chosen to settle too. Although his duties there were administrative, Fletcher was employed by Chicago's Winslow Brothers Company, which produced cast iron and bronze architectural ornament, including significant metalwork for Louis Sullivan. About 1900, Fletcher hired Higginson to design his new house. Still single at the time, his initial housing needs were basic, but he wanted and got something special. This house has been well documented from the time of its construction.

In 1902, the house was published in the *Inland Architect,* and in 1904, it appeared in another article with more photographs entitled "A Small But Spacious Home," in *Architectural Record.* In 1905, *House Beautiful* covered it in a feature called "A Bachelor's Cottage in the Country." These early photographs show that Fletcher had Arts and Crafts furnishings, including some Gustav Stickley pieces, in the living room. They also showed an unusual bullet-shaped pendant light that resembled progressive Viennese designs of that time.

In 1905, Fletcher married Margaret Root, who was the daughter of John Welborn Root, a partner in Burnham and Root, the renowned architects of the Chicago school. Margaret was also an accomplished musician, and the Fletchers used the spacious living room for various entertainments, ranging from piano recitals to Shakespearean plays. Eventually, they had five children, and the house remained in the Fletcher family until the 1950s.

the effect of the Shingle style would significantly trickle down to the fashions of the middle classes.

During the 1880s, as the early Shingle style matured, it became increasingly important in the work of other significant American architects who further developed it. Another established luminary of that field, Henry Hobson Richardson, easily grasped the progressive potential of the Shingle style, as he had earlier with the Romanesque Revival, and others joined him, most notably Peabody and Stearns, and Lamb and Rich, as well as architects such as William Ralph Emerson, Arthur Little, Bruce Price, and John Calvin Stevens. Many of their Shingle-style projects were widely lauded, and some were illustrated in trade periodicals such as *American Builder and Architect* and *Building News.* While a definite influence on the evolution of the Shingle style, some of these homes prefigured elements of the Craftsman style.

It is notable to mention also that the so-called Queen Anne style was well established also by the 1880s as one of the most significant and prominent of the late Victorian era. Emerging just prior to the Shingle style, it rapidly gained popularity across the country, and was a favorite style choice for the latest plan-book house designs. While its overwhelming complexity and sometimes outlandish novelty of its forms and detailing successfully captured the predominant public taste of the moment, it was fated to be the last gasp of Victorian-era design excess. Although the Queen Anne style had developed under entirely separate influences from those that created the Shingle style, the two shared a fundamental material: shingles. Common to most Queen Anne houses, the use of decoratively patterned shingles for exterior siding (often multiple patterns on a single house) articulated different floor levels, or accented other elements, such as their signature tower forms (SEE FIGURES 113 AND 114). The use of ornamental patterning in roof shingling was also popular. So, despite the disparate applications of this material-in-common, it created an early but somewhat uneasy connection between the Queen Anne and Shingle styles. Sharing similar roots with the relatively pared-down, classically inspired design aesthetic of the Colonial Revival style, the early Shingle style found its most suitable alliance there, and both had a purifying influence on the flamboyance of the Queen Anne style.

Like most styles that appealed to a mainstream audience, the Shingle style took its place among the design selections in many plan books, especially after 1900 (SEE FIGURE 107). By this time, full-blown examples of the Craftsman style could be seen, and it soon seemed to eclipse the Shingle style as the more progressive style of the day. Yet, a more apt description is that these two styles cross-pollinated each other for a time, as characteristics of each show up in many homes built before World War I. Even as the Craftsman style waned in the 1920s, the use of shingled walls continued, mostly in a reprise of its old context with the Colonial Revival style in its later examples during that decade.

Figure 116.

LIVING ROOM OF THE FLETCHER HOUSE.

This living room often draws audible gasps from first-time visitors. Entered from the left, the room is centered on a massive brick fireplace with a broad, tapering chimney. A generous wood mantel is supported on large corbels with rounded ends. A balcony adjoining the skylit stairwell overlooks the space from the second floor, and could function as a "musicians' gallery." The most dramatic aspect of this room is its vaulted beamed ceiling. Originally, the areas between the ceiling beams were covered with a plain canvas fabric, whose finished texture offset the room's preponderance of wood. When the ceiling's canvas deteriorated, a stenciled treatment was applied over panels of a pliable insulation board, which replaced the old canvas as the ceiling's finish material. Created and implemented by Mrs. Fletcher's brother in 1925, the stencil design, called a "Running Pine Tree," remains in excellent condition. Reflective metallic paints add vitality and movement as light plays across its surface. In the far corner, a door leads to the kitchen and the recently added family room. There was originally a built-in sideboard under the balcony where the large display cabinet sits.

Figure 117.

DINING ALCOVE OF THE FLETCHER HOUSE.

The effect of soaring space is tamed by the snug dining alcove, which is lined by windows with simple leaded-glass designs in their upper sashes. Variations of these linear designs appear in many other windows of the house, including the taller living room windows to the left. This alcove gives the feeling of a room within a room, somewhat as an inglenook does. A relaxed mix of old and new prevails. Period dining chairs are by Roycroft. Pillows covered in fabric with a William Morris design add interest to the room's large sofas. While unobtrusive modern fixtures serve to uplight the ceiling effectively, the current owners would like to re-create the room's original bullet-shaped pendant lighting fixture. A display shelf also ran around the room at the height where the new lighting fixtures are mounted, which is also scheduled for restoration.

CRAFTSMAN CROSSOVERS, PART III:
TRADITIONAL AMERICANA

Colonial Revival Style

THE COLONIAL REVIVAL STYLE might, at first, seem an unlikely crossover influence on the Craftsman style. Yet many surviving examples prove otherwise, and the presence and importance of each style during the same period is undeniable. A parallel may be drawn between the Craftsman style's early association with homes of progressive design and the Colonial Revival's purifying influence on existing popular domestic taste, such as simplifying the Queen Anne–style. But the roots of the Colonial Revival run far deeper, and its popularity and influence has lasted far longer. In fact, it may lay claim to being the most popular style ever known in America, one that has never really gone away.

The Colonial Revival is among the most evolved of our historic revival styles with a very specific architectural vocabulary that distinguishes most of its examples. Homes built after about 1880 that outwardly display elements of the Classical vocabulary signal the Colonial Revival style (or its influence). Often termed as "traditional" today, such details included columns either round or square with their tops (capitals) in one of the classical orders. Sometimes columns were used with matching pilasters (flattened columns attached to the wall), which helped further link them to the building. The Colonial Revival is also characterized by variety in molding profiles, ranging from simple and delicate to robust and ornate. To further reinforce a home's classical vocabulary,

Figure 118.

DESIGN FOR A HOUSE (CA. 1915).

This plan-book design by Los Angeles architect and 'Bungalow Man" Henry Wilson makes a Colonial Revival statement. The gambrel roof is a primary feature of so-called "Dutch Colonial" houses. With side-facing gables, the roof is supported in front on low classical columns, and covers a recessed, full-width front porch. The matching chimneys anchoring the home and the low railing wall enclosing the front porch, were recommended to be of cobble (river rock). At left, a single-story rear extension contains the kitchen and utility areas. The wooden keystones at the tops of two arched bedroom dormer windows, and the "open-bed pediments" that frame them (so named for the interrupted base of their triangular outline) are Colonial Revival–style details. A row of windows in an adjoining sewing room completes the wide dormer. The estimated cost of this house, which included hardwood floors and box-beamed ceilings in the public rooms, was listed as $4,000.

Figure 119.

HOUSE IN ROCHESTER, NEW YORK (CA. 1920).

This front façade is configured in a shallow U-shape, an unusual form for a Colonial Revival–style home. A vine-covered pergola, detailed with classical columns, shelters an entry courtyard. Balanced by matching chimneys of rough-textured stucco, the flanking pair of forward-projecting gables extends at right angles from either end of a taller part of the house (with side-facing gables) across the rear. The public rooms within the two projecting sections have windows on three sides. Above these, dormer windows set into the steep sides of the gambrel roofs supplement both space and light in bedrooms. Tiny shed-style awnings, diamond-paned sashes, and flower boxes on the small second-floor windows integrate the chimneys into the overall design. The Colonial-style, brick-paved driveway leads to a matching, detached rear garage.

additional low-relief ornamental elements, such as wide decorative borders (friezes), finials, or panels, might be discreetly added. While some of these appeared to be made of carved wood, most were of cast plaster (mixed with straw or horsehair as a binding agent) and protected by thick coats of enamel paint. To help preserve them, such ornaments were usually placed in areas less directly exposed to the elements, such as under the eaves of the roof or porch.

Often achieved largely through the use of symmetry in a home's overall composition, especially in larger-scale examples, this style is predisposed to express a sense of formality. In overall form, most Colonial Revival homes are quite straightforward, and most often rectangular in plan, usually with greater width than depth. Their roof forms are often hipped (pyramidal), or may feature two large side-facing gables (SEE FIGURE 120). Like some other features of the Colonial Revival, the gambrel roof form, associated with so-called "Dutch Colonial" homes (SEE FIGURES 118, 119, AND 122) also crossed over into the Shingle style. The use of projecting dormer windows was especially common (SEE FIGURES 118–124). As was the case in many early historic examples, Colonial Revival chimneys tend to be prominently placed in the middle of one end of the house or the other, sometimes on both. When chimneys are placed at the center of the roof, they recall other actual Colonial examples, whose large, central chimney stacks were part of a passive heating system. Their heated-up bricks emitted gentle warmth into rooms that abutted them.

The most defining feature of many Colonial Revival homes is a centrally placed porch (portico). Depending on the home's scale, these may be one or two stories in height. With detailing adapted from the Greco-Roman temple fronts of classical antiquity, they are often comprised of a triangular, forward-facing gable (pediment) supported by a row of columns (SEE FIGURES 121 AND 124). More modestly scaled examples may have only a simple overhang sheltering the front door, supported by a single pair of columns, or perhaps cantilevered from the wall on brackets of scrolling form. The most characteristic exterior wall finish materials are clapboard siding of narrow width, brick (often red), and occasionally, natural stone. In the context of this style, if shingled walls appeared, they were usually painted.

The door and window frames (casings) of Colonial Revival homes are given more emphasis by the use of wider, more prominent moldings. Within these, the window sash is usually double-hung; rectangular divided panes or "lights" were used, typically numbering from six to eight, and sometimes these only appeared in the window's upper half (SEE FIGURES 118 AND 124). Other windows departed from the grid pattern; among the most popular was a diamond pattern, usually confined to the upper sash (SEE FIGURE 122). For an antique look, leaded glass might be used, otherwise wood mullions would suffice to create the divisions. Other divided-light shapes were also used, such as elongated lozenges (SEE FIGURE 121).

Figure 120.

HOUSE IN BUFFALO, NEW YORK (CA. 1915).

The sense of formality implied by the symmetrical balance in the design of this Colonial Revival home is offset by the rough texture and randomly sized stone blocks of its masonry walls. Incorporating chimneys at their centers, the stone gable ends secure structural support like "bookends" to the attic level. On either side of the chimneys, small quarter-circle windows add interest while lighting the attic rooms. The segmental, arched-topped window openings in the stone walls relieve the design's straight lines and angles. Clad to match the red roofing, the three hipped-roof dormers appear smaller and less conspicuous, as deep colors recede. For this reason, the use of dark-colored paint on the front porch (portico) also reduces its prominence. Colonial Revival-style homes would usually employ a light color to highlight refined porch woodwork detailing and classical columns. The porch roof's metal railing appears to be a later addition.

Figure 121.

BERNAYS HOUSE, LOS ANGELES, CALIFORNIA (1905).

This American foursquare was built as speculative housing by Charles Staples. The architect was Samuel Tilden Norton and photographer Philip Sherman Bernays was the first owner. Combining Colonial Revival with Craftsman style, its square plan, hipped roof, and front-facing dormer are all typical foursquare features. The recessed front porch is less typical, but is the façade's most defining element. With classical detailing and a temple front form inspired by antiquity, it is composed of groupings of squared columns, and crowned by a triangular pediment with scrolling, low-relief decoration. Colonial Revival influence is evident in the lozenge-shaped divisions in the windows' upper sashes, and the dentil molding below the leaded-glass transom of the three-part window. Expressing the Craftsman style are the use of different wall finishes on each floor level, the exposed rafter tails, and the wide, plain window casings. A broad band of trim separates the second floor's shingled walls from the wide clapboard siding of the lower level. The Bernays House has been designated as Los Angeles' Historical-Cultural Monument No. 780.

The Palladian window, named after Andrea Palladio, a renowned Italian Renaissance-era architect, was a popular choice for many Colonial Revival homes. A three-part unit, it consists of a taller central window with a round-arched top, flanked on either side by shorter rectangular windows. Generally used as an accent element rather than repetitively, Palladian windows varied in scale (SEE FIGURE 123). A large version could be used to light a stairway landing (SEE FIGURE 127), while a smaller one might be placed in the peak of a gable to light an attic-level room (SEE FIGURE 122). Another Colonial Revival favorite, also commonly used as an accent but smaller in scale, were oval-shaped windows. An added component of some were leaded-glass (sometimes spider web–shaped) divisions.

For added light, and often more ventilation, transoms were commonly used above front doors, but sometimes above larger windows too. Transom shapes most typical of Colonial Revival homes were half-round arches, or flattened arches, common in "fanlight" transoms. Frequent companions to either side of the front door were narrow vertical windows, called sidelights. As with most homes, the front door was supposed to make a welcoming, style-appropriate statement; Colonial Revival doors feature groupings of recessed panels (usually from four to six). Most are painted an accent color that may not repeat anywhere else on the house, such as a vivid red, deep green, or blue. Some front doors are fitted with glass in their uppermost panels. A key place to express the style of any home, the hardware of the front door was likely to be patterned

after period examples and of substantial scale; an oversized door knocker matching the latch set was a popular companion. Most hardware was made of polished or darkly patinated brass, but a choice for more simply detailed homes might be black-painted wrought- or cast-iron hardware. Except in examples intended to appear rather rough hewn, exposed strap hinges, popular for the front doors of Craftsman style homes, were not common in the Colonial Revival style. Somewhat predictably, white was the most popular color choice for the exteriors of wood-sided Colonial Revival homes. The look of dark-painted shutters (usually black or dark green) against white clapboard siding was thought to be most faithful to actual period examples, which persists to this day.

In lieu of the revealed construction typical of most Craftsman-style homes, those of the Colonial Revival style tend to primly conceal all of their working structure behind a carefully controlled system of ornament. For example, instead of eaves and brackets visibly supporting their roof eaves, they would be more likely to have a refined cornice of composite elements, built up from crown and dentil moldings, underscoring their roof. Rather than by any other visible structural detail, the columns that support Colonial Revival porch roofs express their functional role only by their particular placement. The style's only construction material to be revealed for its own sake is the brick or stone of examples with walls and/or chimneys of masonry construction.

As might be expected, there were many degrees to which crossover homes could be expressed. One Colonial Revival tendency that was applied to some

Figure 122.

SCONEHENGE, PLYMOUTH, MASSACHUSETTS (1910).

*This home's gambrel roof, configured with crossing gables, could be considered either Shingle or Colonial Revival. Its design also hints at the Craftsman style, as the wisteria-draped porch extends as a porte cochère to the left.
Substantial, square, shingle-clad columns are integral with the porch's low, solid railing wall. In the 1920s, another covered porch on the far right side, with a sleeping porch above, was enclosed with French doors and windows that
were fitted into the low-arched openings on three sides. Designating areas of passage, low gables punctuate either end of the front porch like small temple-front pediments. Colonial Revival influence is expressed in the shallow arches,
diamond-patterned upper-window sashes, and three-part Palladian window arrangements that occur in the upper gables. A former bed-and-breakfast, Sconehenge is now a professional design studio and private home.*

Craftsman homes was a use of symmetry in their overall design. To further reflect a blend of both styles, some architects managed to creatively combine oddly diverse style details on the exteriors of crossover homes. For example, structural-looking knee braces might spring from elegantly outlined pediments (upper gable walls), an open-beamed pergola might supplant a front porch (SEE FIGURES 119 AND 123), or classical moldings might appear between exposed Craftsman-style rafter tails. To better understand their mixed stylistic heritage, it can be a useful exercise to try and visually dissect such homes piece by piece.

Some Colonial Revival homes, particularly those that were built during the height of the Craftsman era (circa 1900 to circa 1915), may outwardly appear as text-book examples of the style, but may in fact conceal some surprising interior features that are, instead, decidedly expressive of the Craftsman style. This occurrence is not especially unusual, for both styles enjoyed concurrent popularity. Not necessarily applied to every room, elements of the Craftsman style might appear in those areas of a Colonial Revival–style home where a greater sense of coziness and informality were most desirable, such as a den, library, or game room. Sometimes homeowners of the period placed a selection of Colonial Revival furniture into a decidedly Craftsman-style setting. Regardless of a home's scale, this freedom of combining influences made an appealing option for those whose taste leaned towards the conservative, but were nevertheless drawn to more progressive design statements.

As an especially favorite style choice in the 1920s, Colonial Revival–style plan-book home designs were sometimes known to combine some Craftsman- or Shingle-style influences. Applications to interiors might include Craftsman-inspired built-in cabinetry, a fireplace set into an inglenook, a breakfast nook in the kitchen, box-beamed ceilings, or the millwork styles of entire rooms. Other design opportunities that could blend the styles included lighting fixtures and hardware. Another interior opportunity to blend Colonial Revival and Craftsman influences was in staircase designs. Square newel posts with chunky proportions were quite common to both styles, but more Colonial Revival influence was added by some-times outlining recessed panels on the sides of the post with a period-style molding such as a small-scale "egg and dart" design. The newel post could also be encircled by the same molding below the overhang of its flat cap. Conversely, Craftsman-style newel posts typically had plain recessed side panels or were simply a solid mass of unadorned wood. With or without a newel post, if a Colonial look was desired, the railing spindles were delicately turned in a traditional pattern (SEE FIGURE 127). But if Craftsman style was preferred, the spindles were most usually made plain and square (commonly, about two inches square each). In lieu of any newel post, an alternate was to terminate stair railings, with either turned or square spindles, into a tight spiral that was secured to an outwardly curving bottom step at the foot of the stairs. Instead of spindles, some stair railings employ wide boards, with strategically placed cutout designs in the manner of railings on Swiss Chalets, positioned to create a repeating pattern. Since these kinds of railings are more decorative than plain square-spindled ones, they could integrate the two crossover styles quite effectively.

Concerning the historical sources of the Colonial Revival, it grew out of the popular sentiments first stirred up by America's 1876 Centennial, which encouraged a growing sense of patriotism and nationalism across the country. At its celebratory

Figure 123.

HOUSE IN ROCHESTER, NEW YORK (CA. 1915).

An interesting hybrid design, this house exhibits mostly Colonial Revival elements, with a distinct Prairie influence. The impressive entry porch has arched openings that echo those of the Palladian-inspired windows of the first floor. Its solid roof on classical columns is detailed to resemble an open-beamed pergola, which gives it a lighter effect. The home's overall form, a large rectangular box, has a hipped roof with broadly flaring eaves. Dormers borrow the English Cottage–style, clipped (jerkin-headed) gables. The height of the first story's brick walls, exaggerated by its extension to the sills of the second-floor windows, creates the effect of a broad, Prairie-style frieze encircling the top of the house. Streetside, the frieze has accents of inset brick decoration in square motifs flanking the central row of windows. In a Prairie-style detail, the lightly colored stucco finish is continued, unbroken, onto the underside of the deep eaves.

Elements of the Craftsman style might appear in those areas of a Colonial Revival–style home where a greater sense of coziness and informality were most desirable, such as a den, library, or game room.

Figure 124.

THREE RIVERS FARM, NEW HAMPSHIRE (1901).

Designed by Chapman Frazer as the summer home of the Rollins family, this stunning, fully restored, Colonial Revival mansion is now a year-round home. The view is of the less-formal rear elevation facing the garden and water views. The main building's roof is an oversized gambrel type, with dormers along its length, and side-facing gables with oversized brick chimneys. A projecting, central temple-front portico marks the formal entry, with four classical columns supporting a wide pediment top. On this private side of the house, recessed, sheltered loggias are directly accessed from the central stair halls on both the first and second floors. A pair of single-story covered porches, in the form of small classical temples, expand the usable space of the adjoining living room on the left and dining room on the right, and create an open courtyard space between them.

Figure 125. (opposite)

LIVING ROOM OF THREE RIVERS FARM.

With a stately Colonial Revival—style exterior, the interior surprises visitors with its early original Arts and Crafts features. Entered from the central hall through a wide doorway opposite the fireplace, the living room connects to a smaller hallway through a door on the bookcase-lined wall, and also to the rear outdoor porches. Detailed in Craftsman style, the original high-wainscot paneling and ceiling beams are of solid cypress. The inglenook is lit by leaded-casement windows, and its durable terra-cotta tile floor and red brick walls match the house exterior. A border of Grueby green matte-finish glazed field and ship motif accent tiles is set below the windowsills. Original hand-wrought metalwork includes the wall sconces, hammered copper fireplace hood, and (partly visible at left) large log holder. Renovations added the period pattern wallpaper frieze and the area carpet that reproduces a Morris "honeysuckle" pattern.

exhibition in Philadelphia, the public was newly enchanted by the displays of seventeenth- and eighteenth-century American artifacts, artwork, and period furnishings. Renewing attention to our earliest Colonial years, the event also sparked a reexamination of longstanding traditions of design and architecture. While the legacy of our Colonial era confirms a strong influence of England, the prevailing sentiments of its later revival tended to de-emphasize this connection, and instead play up whatever supported the impression of our forefathers' feisty independence, courage, and supposed good taste.

One of the earliest effects of the Colonial Revival was that it fostered a new interest in American antiques, especially in the context of the collectibles marketplace. During this period, some museums began to rethink how they had been interpreting our own history, which helped lead the way to the assembly of important public and private collections of American decorative arts. Historic surviving homes came under new scrutiny, especially any with direct links to our Founding Fathers, such as George Washington's Mount Vernon. The pressing importance of preserving such sites helped to spur America's historic preservation movement.

A word of caution: some people inadvertently confuse examples of the earlier Greek Revival style (most popular in the second quarter of the nineteenth century) with those of the Colonial Revival. A primary difference is that the earlier style is generally characterized by a more somber sense of restraint. On larger Greek Revival homes, the most ornate elements may be its tall columns and capitals, and other smaller examples are typically well proportioned, but otherwise quite plain in detail. In contrast, Colonial Revival–style homes tend to exhibit a freer use of ornament, and decorative effects in general. In their overall form, they often show a closer kinship to the massing of some of Queen Anne–style homes, especially of multiple gables and hipped roofs. With few exceptions, most Colonial Revival–style homes were and are unlikely to pass for the real thing, for that was not their intention.

While most popular and at home on the East Coast, the Colonial Revival style struck a chord with many Americans across the country, convincing even some of the more progressively-minded to reconsider it. Perhaps opposites do attract, for when a style so based in tradition joined forces with one as progressive as Craftsman, charming and enduring results occurred, some bridging the best of those worlds. By the 1920s, as the Craftsman era waned, the Colonial Revival style became more popular than ever. Fatefully, as that decade progressed, fewer new homes of any style were likely to exhibit more than a lingering trace of Craftsman-style influence.

Figure 126. (opposite)
DINING ROOM OF THREE RIVERS FARM.

The original features of this room such as the hand-wrought central lighting fixture, matching double sconces, and the hand-hammered copper fireplace hood remain intact. The prominent inglenook, and the paneled walls and ceiling milled from old-growth, redwood make this large room quite cozy. Around the top of the brick-lined space is a decorative border of low-relief, ceramic tiles made by Henry Mercer's Moravian Pottery and Tileworks (see Figure 50). The curving end of the built-in bench is a typical Colonial Revival detail. The French doors lead to a covered outdoor porch. An English Arts and Crafts wallpaper pattern of stylized "blackbirds baked in a pie" by C. F. A. Voysey, was re-created for the room's frieze. A richly patterned area carpet adapts another period design by Morris.

Figure 127.
UPPER STAIR HALL OF THREE RIVERS FARM.

A spacious central stair hall with a full-length peaked ceiling bisects two floors of the house front to back. The Palladian window is located directly above the front door, while an open sitting area anchors the other end. Colonial Revival and Craftsman styles combine here naturally. The traditional profiles of the moldings, white-painted trim, raised paneling, and turned stair railing spindles are consistent with the exterior Colonial Revival style. A small casement window opening to the third floor lounging room is configured as dormer, and fitted with Colonial-inspired leaded bottle glass The hall's other aspects, such as the curving truss braces, the mahogany doors, and the wrought-iron hardware follow an Arts and Crafts direction. The wall sconces around the hall are original, but the period chandelier, once lit by both gas and electricity, is a recent addition.

Mission and Spanish Colonial Revival Styles

Their appearances suggest faraway sources but the Mission Revival style, and to some extent the later Spanish Colonial Revival style, can be considered part of the Far West's alternative version of the "other" Colonial Revival discussed earlier in this chapter. Each style is emblematic of a period in our history when a large part of now-American land was under the rule of foreign nations. A further parallel may be drawn from the initial appearance of the Mission Revival style, beginning in the 1890s, for despite the historic connotation of its roots, it can be seen as a reaction to and a major break with the prevailing premise of America's Victorian-era obsession with imported historic revival styles. While most of these had reflected little or nothing of our own country's history, the Mission Revival did reflect an important part of it.

Furthermore, the Mission Revival style can claim a closer connection to the Craftsman style, and links to Arts and Crafts influence, for its period of greatest popularity occurred at the same time as the Craftsman style. Influential tastemaker Gustav Stickley traveled to California in 1904, where he closely observed the newest examples of Craftsman-style bungalows, and the vibrant presence of the Arts and Crafts movement at work. Moreover, Stickley toured some of the surviving remains of California's old missions. Their simplicity, use of natural materials, and honest approach to construction impressed him greatly. He also saw in them an American-born parallel to the imported ideals and tenets of the Arts and Crafts movement that had already so inspired him. Stickley's sturdy, squared-off furniture forms were then likened to some that appeared in actual old mission interiors. However, the widely popular use of the term *Mission* for his furniture's style annoyed him; he always insisted on using *Craftsman*. Both terms persist in popular use today.

In the January 1904 issue of the *Craftsman* magazine, Stickley published design and floor plans for "A Craftsman House Founded on the California Mission style." The accompanying article stated that this "was the first house designed in the Craftsman Workshops," and was being published "for the benefit of the newly formed Home Builders' Club," through which Stickley would ultimately market hundreds of other house plans. The article went on to describe the home's exterior color scheme as a "soft warm creamy tone, almost a biscuit color," and that "while the outside of the house is plain to severity, the inside, as we have designed it, glows with color and is rich in suggestion of home comfort." In other articles and photographs he published later in the *Craftsman*, Stickley would often acknowledge California homes and their architects that aligned with his own Craftsman standards.

The Mission Revival style was born out of a renewed interest in the sometimes primitive Spanish Colonial–era architecture built by Spanish missionaries in territories that now comprise several of our southwestern states, including Texas, New Mexico, Arizona, and California. The style, propelled by the public's perceived romance of the Old West, also was considered a good calling card for attracting tourist dollars. The Mission Revival style coincided with the beginning of California's boom in land development, and tends to be most closely associated with that state's surviving examples of early Mission architecture. But some other interesting links to the Golden State also presaged the new style.

Some have credited the influence of a popular book called *Ramona*, an 1884 novel by Helen Hunt Jackson, with igniting new public interest in the California missions, the lore of their early history, and the movement to preserve and restore their largely ruined sites. In the context of both its Spanish Colonial and Native American cultures, *Ramona* painted a vivid picture of California frontier life. Despite its being fiction, *Ramona* caught the public's imagination, and many readers in search of the sites so convincingly described by Hunt in her book flocked to California as tourists. The resulting commercial opportunities were considerable, and not at all lost on those who saw profit in the romance. The book was given credit for helping to launch the Golden State's fledgling tourism industry, but it also sparked new interest in California's surviving early adobe hacienda-type homes, built around courtyards, prompting adaptations of that planning format both within the state and elsewhere. Some of these early haciendas became almost as admired as the old missions, and such sentiments helped save some from destruction. One such example

Figure 128. (opposite)

LOUNGING ROOM OF THREE RIVERS FARM.

So named on the original plans, this soaring space is in nearly original condition. It shares third-floor space with guest bedrooms. This view shows almost half of the room's overall space, and part of the angled sides of the oversized gambrel roof can also be seen. Located in the side-facing roof gable, a large window grouping (out of view, at right) is centered on the room. Each end of the room has dormer windows with built-in seats. Steep ladder-like "ship stairs" lead to the balcony that overlooks the space on three sides. The balcony railing is whimsically detailed with cutout shapes of the playing card suits. Two fireplaces occupy opposite ends of the room and above each mantel, the playing card suits are cut into the paneling and grouped as a "full house."

Figure 129.

DESIGN FOR A HOUSE (1926).

Called "The Alhambra," this design was published in Honor Built Modern Homes, a plan book of ready-cut homes. The complete package was priced at $3,134. It shares the boxy overall form, hipped roof, and front dormer typical of foursquares, but its stuccoed exterior is Mission Revival style, signalled by the curvilinear outline of the dormer's front parapet wall. Similar parapets also highlight the front porch roof and the shallow projection on the right side containing the staircase and service entrance. The front eaves are notched to allow the dormer's face to be continuous with the front wall. A shed-roof detail on a shallow living room bay continues around the front porch as a decorative overhang. Outlined by moldings, two rectangular panels fill out the second floor of the façade.

is Rancho Guajome, located in rural San Diego County, and visited by Helen Hunt Jackson in 1882. It survives today as a historic house museum.

The idea of promoting California through its history found other outlets. In 1893, at the World's Columbian Exposition in Chicago, amidst an otherwise mostly Beaux Arts–style environment, the Mission Revival-style California Building was designed by important San Francisco Bay Area architects A. Page Brown, A. C. Schweinfurth, and Bernard Maybeck. This made an early and bold statement, giving the style greater national prominence and visibility. At first, it found favor in applications to larger-scale public-building projects such as hotels, train stations, and churches. A remarkable example of such a hotel is the Mission Inn at Riverside, California (1901 and later), designed by Arthur B. Benton (SEE FIGURES 23 AND 109). When the Mission Revival style's application to residential designs began in earnest, these first tended to be grandly scaled estates, but gradually the style was interpreted for more modest dwellings, such as those in plan book designs.

A fascinating example of California's lure and how this was sometimes of benefit to its historical treasures may be seen in the life of Charles Fletcher Lummis (1859-1928). The Harvard-educated East Coast writer, known for his colorful personality, made a literary splash writing about observations and experiences he gathered between 1884 and 1885 while walking the distance between Chillicothe, Ohio, and Los Angeles. After this adventure, he settled in Southern California, becoming city editor of the *Los Angeles Times,* and thereafter expressing much interest in the history of California and the West, particularly the contributions of Native American, Spanish, and Mexican cultures (SEE FIGURE 131). In 1897, his passion for California's history inspired Lummis to found The California Landmarks Club, an organization responsible for starting up the restoration efforts on the early surviving missions. Starting with his own private collection dedicated to the tribal arts and crafts of Native Americans, Lummis went on to establish the Southwest Museum in Los Angeles in 1907, leaving a remarkable legacy.

Begun in San Diego in 1769, California's chain of missions was constructed under the auspices of the Franciscan order, and eventually reached a total of twenty-one. Many of these mission settlements were catalysts for the growth of communities, which eventually became towns and cities, although some mission sites still languish in rural countryside today. Built more or less consecutively, the chain of missions started in the south and gradually moved north as far as Sonoma. Areas were targeted that had significant Native American populations to enlist as converts to Christianity as well as for manual labor. Most missions were located on or close to California's coast and were sited in areas with reliable water supplies and agricultural potential.

Guided by the Franciscan friars, the construction employed adobe bricks manufactured under their stewardship by the Native Americans. Adobe bricks were made from natural clay mixed with bits of straw as a binding agent and sun-dried to a workable hardness. In order to support the considerable weight of the roofs' massive supporting log structure as well as its terra-cotta tile covering, the adobe walls of mission churches and related buildings often required a thickness of up to several feet.

Because of their then-remote locations, no trained architects designed the mission buildings, and some structures are more aesthetically successful than others. Outwardly, their appearance was often less of an intended style statement than a reflection of practical solutions to organizational and functional needs. Nevertheless,

whether from European memories or from seeing other Spanish-built examples elsewhere in the New World, some of the friars must have been familiar with current Spanish architectural fashions. Although most of their adaptations tended to be somewhat crude in comparison, they successfully infused many of their mission buildings with a subtle beauty and harmony.

Other than their whitewashed, irregular exterior adobe walls and handmade red tile roofs, some of the mission architecture's most compelling design elements were fully rounded arches. When used in repetition, they created deeply shaded arcades that stretched alongside various buildings in the mission complex, providing shelter from the elements. Because these arcades were also built of adobe, they needed to be quite thick to support the log timbers of the deep overhangs that formed their shed-style roofs, but not as thick as the supporting walls of the buildings. Some of the most romantic images associated with the old missions are their atmospheric courtyard spaces, especially those ringed by shadowy arcades against walls of irregular adobe. Among the most celebrated of all are the missions at San Juan Capistrano (still partially in picturesque ruins), and at Santa Barbara (often called the most beautiful). These and the other original mission sites are all open to the public.

Besides rounded arches and their application to arcades, some other characteristic forms favored by the friars for their missions were freely adapted in the Mission Revival style. The curving tops adapted from Baroque sources were used on special structures that are often called bell towers, but not the kind that are enclosed buildings. These were adobe structures with arched niches that penetrated their thickness. Almost like small window openings, they housed the mission's bells, which were backlit by the sky. Called *campanarios,* these might be integrated into part of a wall or attached to an enclosed structure as part of its design. Sometimes freestanding, this particular type of bell tower had to be built with enough thickness to support the heavy weight of bronze bells, which in larger examples were used in multiples, with their niches placed in staggered rows at different levels. It was the curving tops of these wide, flat-sided towers that were most commonly translated into the Mission Revival style.

This same curvilinear outline was also translated into a treatment as a decorative roof-gable, sometimes referred to as a parapet, which extended above the actual roofline to create a more interesting silhouette against the sky. In some actual historic mission architecture, this detail was sometimes added as an ornamental flourish to an otherwise plain front façade of the compound's most important building, such as its church. In a typical example, the wall of the front façade is extended upward

(continued on page 127)

Figure 130. (*opposite*)

HOUSE IN SEATTLE, WASHINGTON (CA. 1915).

Distinctly separate forms break up the massing of this house, creating the impression of more modest scale. The most defining feature is the distinctively curving Mission Revival parapet atop a front-facing dormer. The façade's asymmetrical composition and collection of style effects obscures its foursquare form, which is more apparent on the right side. As seen in Figure 129, The left dormer's decorative parapet gains greater prominence from the notch in the front eaves below it, making the dormer's face contiguous with the second-floor walls. Plain square porch columns and simple detailing, the brick-faced first floor, and the simple geometry of the window sash divisions hint of Prairie style. Deeply overhanging eaves and exposed rafter tails are typical Craftsman-style features, but they often appear on Mission Revival homes.

Figure 131.

LUMMIS HOUSE (EL ALISAL), LOS ANGELES, CALIFORNIA (1895-1910).

El Alisal ("the sycamore") was the Highland Park home of Charles Fletcher Lummis. His interest in the Spanish Colonial era, the Franciscan missions, and Native American cultures inspired the style, although there is an underlying Arts and Crafts aesthetic. The rocks were collected from a nearby arroyo. In the dining room façade, the gable is capped by a characteristic curving parapet, adapted from the San Gabriel Mission bell tower. The bell was a gift from the king of Spain. Holding the home's rambling composition together is the picturesque round tower. The house is entered from the other side through a striking set of double front entry doors incorporating Lummis's stylized cipher, designed by artist Maynard Dixon, who also designed some of the home's built-in furniture. It is open to the public as a house museum.

Figure 132.

HOUSE IN DENVER, COLORADO (CA. 1915).

With its romantic "bell tower" and lengthy front porch arcade, this imposing Park Hill house presents a textbook example of Mission Revival style. Linked by a window box, a trio of small-scale windows at the top of the tower echoes the porch's rhythmic arches. Above the porch, a roof deck is accessible from the second floor. The ends of square beams project from its front face, similar to natural log exposed beams (vigas) used in the Southwest's pueblo architecture and a signature component of the Pueblo Revival style (see Figure 137). The Craftsman influence that often crossed over into Mission Revival homes is seen in the multiple divided light grids in the upper sashes of the windows, and the deep overhangs of the hipped red-tile roofs, which feature exposed rafter tails and curving brackets at the outside corners.

Figure 133.

HOUSE IN SPOKANE, WASHINGTON (1909).

In historic South Hill, Swedish native Aaron Lundquist constructed this imposing Mission Revival—style corner home for a dentist named Dr. Bradley. The interiors of this house are mostly detailed in the Craftsman taste. The Mission Revival style is most noticeable in the series of curving parapets that cap its gable ends, which appear to rise up and through the extended eaves, rather than interrupting them (see Figures 129 and 130). The hipped form is applied to various portions of the roof. Exposed rafter tails in the Craftsman mode remain visible underneath the eaves' gutters. Sturdy, round, classical columns support the roof of the commodious front porch. Lower in pitch than the roof above, the porch's eaves are equally deep, and are also detailed with exposed rafter tails. A winterized sleeping porch, with delicately scaled, arch-topped openings, projects over the front entry on the right. Unusual but original accents include the sculptural panel over the front entry, and a smaller panel near the top of the chimney that depicts an American Indian.

past the building's peaked roof gable, screening it from view and terminating in a decoratively scrolled top edge. A famous example of a façade given shape by such a decorative parapet is the Alamo, in San Antonio, Texas. Another Franciscan mission site, it was immortalized by the 1836 massacre of Texans by Mexican forces. Sometimes, like the *campanarios* previously described, some gable-end parapet structures were also pierced by a series of small arched niches to house the mission's bells. The curving tops of similarly shaped parapets are a defining feature of Mission Revival rooflines (SEE FIGURES 129–131, 133–136).

Another form adapted from examples of some original mission architecture was the enclosed bell tower. Typically attached to a church, it was interpreted in a variety of ways. It is notable that most mission sites did not have access to the proper engineering skills or have the resources necessary to construct bell towers of significant height. Therefore the presence of tall, square bell towers in Mission Revival architecture is not always an accurate historic reference. When these did occur on historic churches, their tops were sometimes finished with rounded domes. One of the most imposing elements to be applied to its domestic architecture, the Mission Revival's version of a bell tower is usually square in plan, and most rise above the rest of the house by a full story. Most likely to be hipped in form, and with a red tile roof, some of these towers contain covered, open-air living space at their top, well-ventilated spots for sleeping porches or for admiring the view. Others have fully enclosed rooms ringed by windows (SEE FIGURE 132). This type of square tower is

really more closely related in form to examples of a much earlier vintage, and similar to those found in the countryside of Italy's Tuscany. So-called villas built in the Victorian era's Italianate style, most popular from the 1850s to the 1870s, typically incorporated such square towers. Therefore, as a Mission Revival element, these may be considered as more generically Mediterranean in origin, rather than exclusively derived from Spanish Colonial sources.

Although fueled by similar regional interests, the later Spanish Colonial Revival style differed from the simpler designs and more basic premise of the Mission Revival style. This was a factor in why the earlier style was considered more compatible with an Arts and Crafts sensibility. Jump-started by the success of the style as it was applied to various public buildings designed by noted architect Bertram Grosvenor Goodhue (1869-1929) for the 1915 Panama-Pacific Exposition in San Diego's Balboa Park, the Spanish Colonial Revival was most popular in the Southwest. Examples both commercial and residential were built across the country, mostly in the 1920s and 1930s. Fueled by the style's greater novelty and links to California and Hollywood, it had far more popularity for plan-book designs of that period than did the Mission Revival.

Unlike the Mission Revival's sometimes crude interpretations, the Spanish Colonial Revival style was closely modeled on far more sophisticated examples of seventeenth- and eighteenth- century architecture adapted from European Baroque sources that were built in Central and South America. Although it shared exterior walls of painted stucco and red terra cotta tile roofs of the earlier style, other features

continued on page 136

Figure 134.

HOUSE IN DENVER, COLORADO (CA. 1910).

In an inventive adaptation of the Mission Revival style, this house is made entirely of masonry construction. The brick color even approximates natural adobe. The style's signature curving parapet gable ends are boldly interpreted; they appear improbably large where they comprise the upper outline of the entire side of the house. Their effect continues, in part, to the rounded-arch opening at the sides of the front porch. On the front-facing dormer, the three-part arrangement with a taller arch-topped window between two lower square-topped ones, recalls the Palladian window form favored by the Colonial Revival style. Exposed rafter tails under the angled eaves lend a Craftsman-influenced detail. Similar square beams extend to support a small balcony in front of the dormer, whose coiling iron railing further references the Spanish influence.

Figure 135. (opposite)

HOUSE IN SANTA BARBARA, CALIFORNIA (CA. 1915).

This house is made more impressive by its prominent exposure on a corner lot. A grand example of a Mission Revival home, it features two primary side-facing gables, with the typical concept of a curving-top parapet on the gable ends expanded to near its limit, however, the form does not repeat elsewhere on the building. A square tower with a hipped tile roof is at the outside corner. Pairs of round columns support the porch overhangs, while larger eaves support the open-beamed roof of an attached pergola. A pair of small arched windows on the large side gable implies a third opening between them. In the upper window sashes, crossing ogee (double-curved) lines create a distinctive pattern of generous divisions in scale with such a large house. After a disastrous earthquake in the mid-1920s wiped out most of Santa Barbara's predominantly Victorian-era commercial district, the city adopted the Spanish Colonial Revival vernacular as its thematic architectural style. This has proven aesthetically and commercially successful for a city that thrives on tourism.

Figure 136.

HOUSE IN SAN DIEGO, CALIFORNIA (1912).

This Mission Revival house was designed by architect William Wheeler for Mary Rhinehart. With vertical walls seeming to pass through the roof eaves, the right tower roof detailing is similar to Figure 133. Here the curving parapet form is adapted to the top of the tower element, and also on the pro-jected front porch, where it is expressed in two distinct places above flattened arched openings. Suggested by the potted plants, there is some usable deck space on the porch roof. The signature pink sidewalks are a distinguishing, original feature of the city's historic Burlingame district. Garnished with a scattering of river rock, Mediterranean plantings in the front landscape are a style-appropriate choice. San Diego was not only the site of the first California eighteenth-century mis-sion, it is also the official birthplace of the Spanish Colonial Revival style that emerged in the wake of the popularity of the still-existing, signature buildings of the 1915 Panama-Pacific Exposition in the city's famous Balboa Park.

Figure 137.

HOUSE IN PASADENA, CALIFORNIA (CA. 1920).

Adapting southwestern Native American architecture, this house exemplifies the Pueblo Revival style. Features generally include a flat roof, thick walls with battered (sloping) sides, and projecting beams (vigas) sometimes left in their natural state. Only Mission Revival offers any similarity, as each makes reference to the regional Native American tradition of mud-brick (adobe) construction, augmented by simple wood framing. Neither Spanish colonials or Native Americans were a major influence on the domestic architecture of the other, and the Pueblo Revival's early-twentieth-century appearance was primarily a result of its novelty. More regionally limited than Mission Revival, the Pueblo Revival style was mostly used for public buildings, such as hotels or roadside architecture catering to tourists, than it was for homes. Its primitive informality and close-to-nature appeal also parallels that of the Rustic style, and therefore can claim some sympathetic resonance with Arts and Crafts ideals.

Figure 138.

MOUNT WOODSON CASTLE (AMY STRONG CASTLE),
RAMONA, CALIFORNIA (1916-1921).

Amy Strong, a well-traveled, wealthy fashion designer and manufacturer of gowns for the area's elite, built this home of mostly Spanish and Mission influences. She collaborated with important local architects Emmor Brooke Weaver and John Terrell Vawter. They utilized local granite boulders for thick masonry walls, which tempered the interiors from seasonal heat. Construction timbers were locally grown eucalyptus logs. Also utilized were adobe bricks, British-made chimney pots, and handmade terra-cotta floor and roof tiles. The windmill was inspired by those Strong had seen in Holland, and pumped the water supply. The famous local horticulturalist Kate Sessions originally developed the landscaping. The house's eclectic mélange of influences, construction techniques, and decorative effects extends to its twenty-seven-room interior, where unusual fireplaces, oddly shaped spaces, and curious wall paintings abound. The fate of the house was secured when the estate developed into a golf club and condominium complex, with this building as its centerpiece. Now called Mount Woodson Castle, it is publicly accessible as a venue for gatherings and special events.

The Spanish Colonial Revival style was closely modeled on sophisticated examples of seventeenth- and eighteenth-century architecture adapted from European Baroque sources that were built in Central and South America.

Figure 139.

FERRIS-GRAVES HOUSE, SPOKANE, WASHINGTON (1906).

Architect C. Ferris White designed this South Hill home for Frank and Maud Ferris Graves (no relation to the architect). Symmetry guided the composition of the rear façade, viewed here. While arches are absent, the hipped red-tile roof, white stucco walls, and round columns on the rear porch suggest a Mission Revival influence. Originally the textured stucco walls were left in their more subdued, "natural" finish. The primary public rooms are toward the back, with the dining room on the left and living room at right with a large central hall between them. An angled service wing is on the left, with another angled wing for the family bedrooms on the opposite side. Despite its 5,600 square feet, not including the full basement or attic, this house is technically a "true" bungalow, for its bedrooms and primary living spaces share the same level. With windows under the eaves, the attic was planned as expandable living space. Frank Graves was a prominent local attorney, and this house was designed as the setting for large social gatherings.

Figure 141.

DOOR HARDWARE OF THE FERRIS-GRAVES HOUSE.

In a detail of the inner front door's latch (in Figure 140), the fine quality and striking design of the handcrafted metalwork is fully revealed. Deriving form from function, the latch is a model of good Arts and Crafts design. The working parts of the latch are quite plainly expressed in durable steel with a darkened finish. The projecting handle with the rounded end is lifted to release the pivoting copper bar from the separate catch mounted at left. With a more decorative flourish, the distinctively pierced copper back-plate design incorporates the initials of Frank Graves, the home's original owner. Artfully abstracted, the composition of voids and solids recalls the cutouts in a stencil pattern. This same latch design reappears on some of the other interior doors.

Figure 140.

ENTRY DETAIL OF THE FERRIS-GRAVES HOUSE.

This inner door opens into the entry hall from a roomy vestibule for the front door, which helps conserve heat and block drafts during cold weather. Of quarter-sawn oak to match other woodwork, the door has divided lights in its upper half, and its arrangement of sidelights and a transom mirrors that of the all-wood front door. The entry hall's other features include handsomely detailed box beams, refined coved moldings, and a paneled wainscot, which also extends into the front vestibule. Replicating its original treatment, each wainscot panel is inset with a burlap-textured fabric, and painted with a mottled finish in harmony with the wood. On the upper walls and ceiling, similar paint hues appear in lighter values. Light fixtures, which are not original but of a similar period, are fitted with hand-blown art-glass shades with stylized leaf designs in the Art Nouveau mode.

Figure 142.

LIVING ROOM OF THE FERRIS-GRAVES HOUSE.

This living room looks similar to one in many Craftsman-style bungalows except for its size (more than 1,000 square feet); only half of the entire room is shown here. Extra-wide, built-in bookcases flank the fireplace; those with glass doors on the far left wall are also built in, but closely resemble freestanding furniture. Unexpected but quite practical, a tall-case clock at its center is integral with the design. On the opposite wall, a trio of large windows overlooks the near lawn (see Figure 139). The fireplace surround, faced in matte-finished tiles attributed to Pasadena tilemaker Ernest Batchelder, has a pair of low-relief tile panels on either side. In the 1920s, the Ferris family replaced the original, simpler tile facing, but kept the original architect-designed handcrafted iron-and-copper hood and low fire screen. The paired windows above the bookcases on the fireplace wall expand on a typical Craftsman-style interior feature. The horizontal line above the mantel and bookcases continues around the entire room as the top of a five-foot-high wainscot.

Figure 143. (opposite)

DINING ROOM OF THE
FERRIS-GRAVES HOUSE.

With its fourteen-foot vaulted ceiling outlined in dark-stained oak beams, this is the most dramatic room in the house. Viewed here from its primary entrance off the central hall, the room retains the original set of architect-designed Arts and Crafts dining furniture. The angle-cornered table is well-crafted and artfully proportioned, as are the dining chairs with through-tenon detailing at their upper backs and on their leg stretchers, where they are "keyed." The period style ceiling fixtures replace the missing originals. The Craftsman-style, built-in sideboard, recessed between a pair of windows, has some unusually shaped handcrafted hardware, and is flanked by period sconces. To the left, a small, recessed display cupboard has glass doors matching those on the sideboard. Atop the high wainscoting, a plate rail continues around the room. Under the windows at left are original, handcrafted metal screens designed to conceal radiators. The small copper metallic-finish ornaments resemble those on the living room's fireplace screen. Toward the right is a door leading to the kitchen and service areas.

Figure 144.

STAIRWAY OF THE
FERRIS-GRAVES HOUSE.

These Craftsman-style stairs descend from the main hallway near the living room to the basement. Alternating among the railing's plain square spindles are wider boards with narrow, decorative cutout designs. At the bottom of the steps, a wide hall leads to the billiard room (to the left). Because of the receding slope of the site, this portion of the full-floor basement level is mostly above grade. The volume of space and natural light disguises the feeling of a basement, which elsewhere contains utility and storage areas. Because of their placement in the thicker foundation wall, the lower pair of windows has a display shelf above them. A minor addition to a bedroom above required the left side of both pairs of windows to be blocked. To help offset this loss, their casings and sashes were preserved, and their glass was replaced with mirrors.

continued from page 127

specific to the Spanish Colonial Revival style veered into more complex territory, both inside and out (SEE FIGURE 138). Often included was a lavish use of colorfully glazed ceramic tile on floors, steps, and fireplace surrounds, as well as decorative wrought iron for gates, window grilles, lighting fixtures, and hardware.

Some examples have a decidedly Moorish flavor that reflects the Islamic influence in medieval Spain. Features including courtyards with fountains, parabolic-arched windows and doorways, and geometric tile patterns are all derived from that source. On their exteriors, larger-scale examples of the Spanish Colonial Revival style, both commercial and residential, tend to favor complex building forms. These may include elaborate multistory towers and variously sized domes covered with brightly glazed mosaic tile decoration. A good example of this style on a very grand scale is Hearst Castle (La Cuesta Encantada) in San Simeon, California. The work of the noted architect Julia Morgan (1872–1957), it was built for William Randolph Hearst in phases, mostly in the 1920s and 1930s, and is open to the public as a house museum. Other significant examples of the Spanish Colonial Revival, especially larger churches, display high-relief, sculptural decoration on their façades. Adapted from similar Baroque-style work by José Churriguera, a noted eighteenth-century Spanish architect, the style term "churrigueresque" is sometimes assigned to them.

The fact that such elaborate, higher-caliber structures weren't really built in eighteenth-century California (or elsewhere on American soil) is one reason why their early-twentieth-century revival was considered by some as less authentic to the Golden State or to America. Some argued that the Spanish Colonial Revival style was a disingenuously showy expression of an invented historic past that never even existed on our soil, and that only the Mission Revival had any ring of honesty to it. After all, the original missions weren't built much before the time when California was still believed to be a large island. Its remoteness had helped defer the inevitable onslaught of Spanish exploration and settlement that had already occurred elsewhere to the south, as early as the sixteenth century, in Mexico and Central and South America. It wasn't until 1701 that Baja California was officially confirmed to be a long peninsula attached to the northern mainland, and Gaspar de Portola's first exploratory expedition and the founding of the first mission didn't occur until 1769. But ultimately, such arguments fade in light of the vitality that both the Mission Revival and Spanish Colonial Revival contributed to American domestic design, for each took vestigial remnants of a distant Spanish culture and made them decidedly American statements.

Figure 145.

BILLIARD ROOM OF THE FERRIS-GRAVES HOUSE.

Part of the wide hallway that leads to the stairs in Figure 144 can be seen through the door to the right. Because this basement room is above grade, the pair of windows that flank the simple fireplace admit unexpected light and views, with additional windows on the wall to the left. The extra depth of the window sills, which double as display shelves, is a result of the foundation wall's extra thickness. Faced with small, plain terra-cotta tiles, the fireplace surround highlights an original handcrafted Arts and Crafts copper-and-iron hood. Craftsman-style woodwork detailing, including box beams and high wainscoting, contribute appropriate horizontality to the room. While the comfortable space functions well as a billiard room, it is easy to imagine it as the original owner's home office.

CRAFTSMAN CROSSOVERS, PART IV:
IMPORTING THE PAST

Tudor Revival Style

MORE THAN ANY OTHER FOREIGN INFLUENCE on our culture, England has been important and consistent. The long evolution of our Tudor Revival style that began in the 1880s and faded in the 1930s epitomizes America's interest in British traditions. The influence from England's Arts and Crafts movement came close on the heels of the Tudor Revival's emergence in our country, and inspired some examples to become Anglicized versions of Arts and Crafts homes. Once on American shores, the "medievalizing" influence of the movement, as perpetrated earlier in England by William Morris and his followers shifted its focus. Here, it was less about preserving craft traditions or improving the lives of disadvantaged factory workers, than it was about simply pursuing picturesque English architecture and design through a lens of fantasy; for the Tudor Revival style invented a distant past in a domestic style that had never existed in America.

Because the Tudor Revival occurred over such a considerable time period, its different phases were reflected in variations of some characteristics. In its earliest American incarnation, it was introduced as one of several aspects of diverse inspiration of the so-called

Figure 146.

DESIGN FOR A HOUSE (1929).

This modest home's complex form, from a plan book called Small Homes of Distinction: A Book of Suggested Plans, *is comprised of only three primary rooms on each floor. Its typical Tudor Revival elements include half-timbering, a steeply pitched gabled roof, shallow eaves, and dormer windows. The roof at left, with a shed-roofed dormer lighting the staircase, dips low to cover the entry hall projection, and a second dormer with a hipped roof extends through a break in the eaves. At far right, the roof sweeps down to cover a side porch that adjoins the living room. A massive chimney rises through a shed-roofed extension of an inglenook in the living room. An attached pergola is off the kitchen's rear service porch at left. With their highly visible roofs, most Tudor Revival style homes are significantly enhanced by the use of slate.*

Figure 147.

HOUSE IN SPOKANE, WASHINGTON (1913).

This South Hill Tudor Revival home was designed by prominent local architect Kirtland Cutter for the Nuzum family. It has more vertical proportions that most, and rises to a full three stories, plus an attic level. Extending to the top of the second floor windows, the texture and pattern of the brick facing reduces this perceived height, by implying a taller first floor (set on a high basement), with only one full floor above it. At right, a covered brick porch has suppressed round-arch openings. Extending from under a projecting third floor gable is an open-beamed pergola with an added solid roof covering. While front porches and pergolas were not historically in the Tudor vocabulary, here they are successfully adapted. On the third floor and attic levels, fairly simple half-timbering patterns unite the overall composition, and highlight the multiple gables.

Figure 148.

F. HOLLAND DAY HOUSE, NORWOOD, MASSACHUSETTS (1859; AS REMODELED, 1891–93).

This corner house was originally built by Lewis and Anna Day in the Second Empire style, and sported that style's signature Mansard roof. When their only child Fred Holland Day (1864-1933) hired architect J. Williams Beal to transform the family home, all traces of its former style were obliterated, and this rambling, gabled Tudor Revival emerged. Day was a noted and sometimes controversial fine art photographer, and a partner in the literary publishing firm of Copeland & Day. With refined detailing and half-timbering applications, the home's exterior includes some smaller carved stone elements. Most of the windows have leaded patterns, and some have colored, art-glass insets. A deep wraparound front porch dominates the first floor. Its roof continues to the right as a porte-cochère and, with oddly peaked copper sheathing, terminates in a half-octagonal end. Designed as fully cantilevered, this end recently required supplemental support from two temporary posts at right. Some of the Day family's artifacts and furnishings remain and it is open to the public as the home of the Norwood Historical Society, and a house museum.

Queen Anne style. Improbably, most examples had remarkably little in common with that of England, where it was called Queen Anne Revival. Usually rendered in red brick with white-painted trim, England's version was largely inspired by the seventeenth-century mix of Dutch and English influences on buildings during the namesake monarch's early eighteenth-century rule. In contrast, most examples of America's Victorian-era Queen Anne style were characterized by an asymmetrical and sometimes rambling approach to the massing of somewhat irregular forms. These were typified by rounded corner towers, bay windows of various shapes, wraparound porches, and complex hipped and gabled rooflines. Instead of brick (except for foundations, and chimneys, which sometimes had decorative brickwork) the majority here were constructed of wood. Walls covered with multiple patterns of decoratively cut shingles, as well as an abundance of fanciful wood turnings and other trim further defined our Queen Anne style.

The diverse nature of such a style allowed room for considerable variation driven by the whims of the architect or the homeowner. The diversity of American Queen Anne style homes was a hallmark of the style. In a quiet foreshadowing of its implications, few people at the time took notice when some Queen Anne style homes by the 1880s began to incorporate areas of half-timbering, as that English Tudor Revival element is commonly known, into their already eclectic designs. While the concept of half-timbering is generally agreed to be the original inspiration behind the linear "stick work" applied to the exteriors of homes in the Stick/Eastlake style that immediately preceded it, the half-timbering in some

Queen Anne crossover homes became more literally more *English* in its interpretation (SEE FIGURE 148).

Considered the most signature effect of the Tudor Revival style, half-timbering derived its distinctive appearance from its origins as part of a basic structural building system employed in medieval and early Renaissance-era England, as well as elsewhere in Europe. Thought of as an integral part of its finished design and also foreshadowing an Arts and Crafts sentiment, the building's supporting structural timber frame was left exposed on the exterior walls, and often inside as well. Historically, the various spaces between these timbers were first filled in with a mixture called daub, and then a plaster or stucco finish was applied. Alternately, more elaborate structures used mortared bricks, usually laid in some kind of decorative pattern such as herringbone or basket weave, to fill in between the timbers (SEE FIGURE 152).

In both historic and Tudor Revival examples of half-timbering, the exposed wood was darkly stained rather than painted, providing a sharp contrast to wall areas that were usually painted a light neutral color (or were whitewashed). Some early twentieth century Tudor Revival examples were enhanced with irregularly textured plaster effects and "faux painting" techniques to mimic the look of great age. Exposed structural timbers became a decorative, graphically bold element of the building, and in early historic examples, configurations of half-timbering reflect its utilitarian nature. In more costly designs, these were artfully augmented with additional wood pieces (sometimes curving or carved) to create complex, highly-contrasting overall patterns. A departure from Arts and Crafts tenets, it is important to realize that the vast majority of Tudor Revival style homes regardless of their date employed thin surface-mounted boards, instead of real structural timbers, to achieve their half-timbered effect.

Once it began to be perceived as a valid style rather than a mere adjunct to another, the Tudor Revival was more fully and freely expressed, and its popularity steadily grew. In general outline, the earliest American examples of the style resembled Queen Anne homes, but half-timbering was applied with a generous hand. At this point, American taste wasn't particularly preoccupied with creating authentic, academically correct replicas of period homes, but eventually in some later and especially grander examples, there was sometimes an obsessive quest for authenticity.

While not every Tudor Revival home can claim it, the style's particular association with an Arts and Crafts sensibility came to pass in varying degrees, largely dependent on the skill and inclination of architects. However, the education of American architects had improved by the early twentieth century, and because of their greater exposure to foreign building projects through books, trade journals, and periodicals, most were aware of the connection of England to the origins of the Arts and Crafts movement. In addition, many architects, especially those designing high-end homes, were familiar with, and admirers of, the wallpapers, fabrics, furniture and other decorative work of Morris & Co., some of which remained in production for many years after the 1896 death of William Morris. Furthermore, the well-published work of the next generation of British Arts and Crafts architect/designers, including C. R. Ashbee (1863–1942), M. H. Baillie Scott (1865–1945), Edwin Lutyens (1869–1944), and C. F. A. Voysey (1857–1941), exerted quite a wide influence on concurrent American domestic architecture and interiors.

Separate from the Tudor Revival style's inherent and convenient parallels to the revealed construction tenets of the Arts and Crafts movement, it was certainly Gustav Stickley's favorable impressions of England and Morris that played a primary role in his frequent adaptation of Tudor Revival style references in so many of his Craftsman style home designs. However, almost all the interiors of these homes, whether they were by Stickley or others then designing in the Craftsman mode, reflected typical Craftsman style proportions and included all its characteristic features. So inside most of the predominantly Craftsman-influenced examples, any specifically English references were less likely to be found except in higher budget, custom-built homes. After the Craftsman era faded from fashion, examples of more fully integrated Tudor Revival–style homes that reflect that style both inside and out became far more common in homes of all sizes.

Of all the crossover styles ever blended with Craftsman, it is significant to note that none proved more popular than the Tudor Revival, and few were as aesthetically compatible. Unlike some of the other styles that could seem at odds with Craftsman principles, the best examples of this blend exude an almost seamless, natural fusion. As did many of their historic models, homes of Tudor Revival influence have a rather

(continued on page 147)

Figure 149.

GREAT HALL OF THE DAY HOUSE.

This exceptional vertical space rises three stories (33 feet) to a shallow, barrel-vaulted ceiling. Above its terra-cotta colored walls, the ceiling is divided by a curving grid of beams, where original panels of gold leaf have since darkened. The chandelier, lit by gas, was fueled through the pipe that suspends it from the ceiling. Backlit by daylight through leaded windows, a grand oak staircase (located opposite the far wall) ascends to where this view was taken. A second floor balcony (not visible) extends the entire length of the left wall, and complements the smaller one on the third floor seen at upper left. Conceptually, the space recalls an open courtyard, functioning as a first floor sitting room with a fireplace, and as the home's main circulation space. Interior casement windows overlook it and, help control air movement. With European character, each window sash is fitted with leaded, Flemish bull's-eye glass that catches points of light.

Figure 150.

DINING ROOM INGLENOOK OF THE DAY HOUSE.

Paneled in richly figured Honduran mahogany, this room is lighted from floor-to-ceiling leaded windows at left, parts of which are inset with hand-painted, art-glass panels depicting historic French royalty. Set into a window corner, this handsome inglenook has an early Arts and Crafts sensibility. A broad, flattened Tudor arch frames built-in cushioned seats on either side. The unusual fireplace is built of narrow-profile Roman brick. The central portion of an oversized sandstone lintel flares outward from the fireplace opening, with abstracted organic leaves carved along its edges. On the rear wall, the curved surface activates light on the reflective metallic gold finish of the original, low-relief, Lincrusta Walton wall covering of large, stylized poppies, which has a texture resembling hand-tooled leather. The front parlor beyond at right was the only interior room whose configuration survives intact from the home's first Second Empire style incarnation. As decorated by Fred Day, its features include classical, cream-colored woodwork; original, fitted (wall-to-wall) carpet; and silk damask, fleur de lis wall covering. A wide closeable door to the front parlor, disguised as a paneled wall when open (or closed), is seen at right.

Figure 151.

HOUSE IN PORTLAND, OREGON (1907).

Architect Emil Schacht achieved a strong street presence for this Tudor Revival home built on a narrow lot for Max Loewenson. The over-hanging, half-timbered upper gables, and the projecting central bay and porch, are advanced by their deep eaves. Each gable has an added pointy peak. The lower edges of each fascia board (bargeboard) has been scalloped and notched, adding curves in a rhythmic movement that echo those in the diagonal braces of the half-timbering. Keyed tenons along the bargeboards, each aligned with a rafter tail behind it, are a Craftsman-style detail. The basement-level garage is a later addi-tion. The home's pebbledash stucco facing, a traditional finish of English architecture, appeared on some Arts and Crafts-era homes. Its beauty lies in its simple practicality, for it requires no painting and has a pleasing natural texture and neutral color.

Figure 152.

WICKS HOUSE IN BUFFALO, NEW YORK (1897).

A sophisticated blending of Tudor and Craftsman style influences, this home also anticipates the Prairie style in its massing. Its wood-framed, projecting front porch is where the Craftsman influence is most pronounced. The simple, arching brackets that spring from its corner posts subtly echo the curving cross-braces in the half-timbering above. This home's substantial presence is forcefully expressed in its first floor stone wall masonry, which rises up to a row of small corbels made from irregular stone blocks. Faced in narrow-profile Roman brick that lends a muted horizontal texture, the brick is overlaid in an arrangement of vertical boards relieved only by the cross-braces on either side that create the effect of half-timbering. A trio of dormers with exaggerated peaks caps the high-pitched hipped slate roof. Located in the Parkside area laid out by Frederick Law Olmstead, this house was designed by William Sydney Wicks as his own home, and included a ballroom on the attic level. Wicks worked in partnership with E.B. Green (Green and Wicks), and their firm designed numerous homes and landmark public buildings in Buffalo.

Figure 153.

HAHN HOUSE, PORTLAND OREGON (1905).

Sited on a hillside with city outlooks, this imposing home was designed by noted Portland architect Emil Schact for Henry Hahn. The house is a fine crossover example of the Craftsman and Tudor Revival styles. Supported on large, paired brackets, the spacious attic level's two forward-facing gables extend over two-story bay windows. Below insets of half-timbering on the gable faces, the tops of the paired brackets continue as small corbels repeating across each gable's width. Skewered by Gothic style finials at their peaks, the gable eaves are faced with wide bargeboards, with Gothic-inspired spear-shaped ends, and quatrefoil (four-leaf-clover) cut-out openings along their lengths. Most strongly expressed in the shingled walls with alternating courses, the Craftsman style is seen in the exposed rafter tails of the hipped porch roof, and the groups of bracketed square columns that support it. The front porch adjoins open terraces on either side, which connect on the left to an open-beamed pergola adjoining the dining room.

Figure 154.

FRONT DOOR OF THE HAHN HOUSE.

With a design consistent with Craftsman and English influences, the scale of this front door and sidelight seem quite modest for such a large dwelling. Set against the dark brown, shingled courses of the walls, the cream-colored trim paint used elsewhere pops out the ensemble. The traditional molding profiles around its perimeter lend more refinement. A Tudor Revival influence, the ironwork of the non-functional, long-pointed strap hinges and curvilinear iron window grill has a Gothic feeling. The Craftsman-style door utilizes oak planks secured by butterfly key tenons that span their closely fitted, beveled edges. The sidelight has a delicate grid of leaded squares fitted with beveled glass panels. "Butterfly key" tenons appear between the door's vertical planks (also seen in Figure 156). Inside the door is an entry vestibule, with a second door to the entry hall.

> Of all the crossover styles ever blended with Craftsman, it is significant to note that none proved more popular than the Tudor Revival, and few were as aesthetically compatible.

Figure 155.

HOUSE IN LOS ANGELES, CALIFORNIA (CA. 1910).

Architect Frank M. Tyler here expressed both the Tudor Revival and Craftsman styles in an exuberant, multi-layered assemblage. Half-timbering lends greater prominence to its abundant gables, where paired brackets are placed at slightly staggered heights, next to the curving inside edges of the wide bargeboards. Also at differing heights, attic windows have hexagonal motifs in their divided lights. Similarly detailed side-facing gables are out of view. Set on chunky, square stone columns, a lower gable's spreading roof pitch is slightly lower than in the upper gables, and reinforces the first floor's horizontality. The color scheme contrasts areas of white with green-stained shingled walls, neutral olive gray trim, and soft yellow window sashes. The house is located in the historic West Adams district.

Figure 156.

ENTRY HALL (TOWARD DINING ROOM) OF THE HAHN HOUSE.

Because of open sight lines, portions of all three public rooms that span the home's front façade are visible in this view. This view is from one end of an oversized living room, with windows on three sides, that extends past a central fireplace for the full depth of the house. A grand staircase (out of view) is flanked by doors to rear service areas opposite the glass-paneled, inner front door to the entry vestibule at center. Below the frieze area, a shelf supported by small corbels continues around the entry hall. Alternately, the living and dining rooms each have coved ceilings. Colonial Revival influence is evident in the classical motifs of the entry hall's ceiling plasterwork and the curving end of the built-in bench under the triple window. On the back of the bench and on the base of the colonnade, "butterfly key" tenons (like those in Figure 154) are a Craftsman-style detail. Off the dining room at the far end, French doors are open to a pergola-covered patio area partly seen in Figure 153. The detailing of the colonnade in the foreground matches that of the front porch columns; below their brackets, wall sconces were once mounted.

(continued from page 141)
steep roof, often with multiple gables, and dormers may appear. These features dovetailed particularly well with larger-scaled, predominantly Craftsman style homes, for multiple gables allowed greater prominence of typical supporting brackets beneath their deep overhangs, which were sometimes embellished with English-derived carving or detailing. Wide fascia boards (bargeboards), which face the gable roof's narrow edges, were already common to both the Tudor Revival and Craftsman styles; in crossover homes, these were accented with various decorative treatments along their lengths (including applied decoration, cutout designs, and sometimes carving), to further reinforce an English feeling (SEE FIGURES 151, 153 AND 155). However, the most common of all Tudor Revival details used on primarily Craftsman style homes of all sizes were, in spite of their dubious structural value, half-timbering effects (SEE FIGURES 146–148, 151–153, 155 AND 157).

Despite its easy compatibility with earlier Craftsman-era structures, the 1920s is widely considered to be something of a golden age for America's Tudor Revival style. Frequently applied to smaller bungalows and other relatively modest middle class dwellings, it was the particular vogue for the style as it was applied to very upscale homes

especially during that decade that earned it the soubriquet "Stockbroker Tudor."

It was in this period of the style's evolution in America that a distinct turn towards greater interest in the pursuit of historic authenticity occurred. For well-traveled architects and their clients alike, England's historic manor houses became practical models of study and emulation; serious interest in collecting antique English furniture and other decorative arts from various periods was also afoot, and many obsessive collectors desired and demanded sympathetic surroundings for their treasures. A lingering Arts and Crafts aspect to the Tudor Revival continued to evolve.

By the 1920s, it was almost a matter of necessity that architects wanting to secure the finest projects had to be fully armed with a thorough understanding and working knowledge of not just one, but of several historic revival styles popular during that decade. As evidence of their greater sophistication, some architects gave a nod, if not a direct reference, to the English Arts and Crafts taste in new Tudor Revival–style homes. Where subtlety had greater impact, this was most likely to occur somewhere in their interiors. Such a seasoned design perspective was far more critical to the success of designs for larger-scale, custom-built home projects, than to those routinely produced as plan-book offerings for which unauthorized copying of others' designs was quite common. Especially in large, developer-built housing tracts, it was not unusual to find examples of Tudor Revival–style homes that display their Englishness only on their exteriors; often, the interiors can be plainly conventional with vaguely traditional detailing, lacking commitment to any particular style.

Because it was historically appropriate but also extremely durable, natural slate tiles were the most preferred material to cover the steep gabled roofs of Tudor Revival homes. As a gesture of economy, some designs had roof configurations that allowed for only parts of the roof most visible from the street to utilize slate, while other less conspicuous areas could get by on far cheaper roofing materials such as composition shingles, preferably of a compatible color and texture. Sometimes, prominent front dormers were given slate coverings on their sides, as well as on their roofs. Because of considerable expense, slate roofs were a much less likely feature of smaller-scale bungalows. Although they occur on many Craftsman crossover examples, the most authentic Tudor Revival designs were not likely to have much, if any, front porch. Alternatively, a smallish overhang with suitably styled posts or bracket supports, sometimes sheltered front doors. Others were recessed into the front wall, to create a shallow, covered entry vestibule instead.

Figure 157.

ADAM J. MAYER HOUSE, MILWAUKEE, WISCONSIN (1905).

Overlooking Lake Michigan, this home was designed by architect Henry G. Lotter, for Adam J. and Pauline Mayer. An open porch under an awning adjoins the covered entry porch. Their son Frederick and his wife Elizabeth occupied this house until 1971, so many of the exceptional interiors were preserved. The Tudor Revival style home sits on a narrow urban lot that necessarily placed most of its exterior interest on the front façade, and dictated a design with vertical emphasis. On the first floor to the right, art glass in the upper sashes of the double windows of the library is visible. This was part of the interior design work of important Milwaukee interior and furniture designer George Mann Niedecken in 1907. The firm of Niedecken-Walbridge, Inc. specialized in complete interior design services, including the manufacturing, and installation of custom-designed furniture, textiles, art glass, and lighting fixtures. Niedecken collaborated with Frank Lloyd Wright on the interiors and furnishings of some of Wright's most significant projects including the Avery Coonley and Frederick Robie houses (1908-1910) and the Bogk house (see Figures 101-106).

Figure 159.

STAIRWAY (FROM ENTRY HALL) OF THE MAYER HOUSE.

This view shows the part of the entry hall that was obscured by the stairway railing in Figure 158. The overhanging flat cap of the newel post is a detail used in some British Arts and Crafts furniture. The attenuated "V" shapes of steeply angled spindles in the railing create a subtle sense of movement. Art-glass windows at the landing admit daylight from the side of the house. Niedecken utilized the angle of the upper stairway to develop a triangulated design for the wall area beneath it, which adjoins the library to the right. The entry hall's wainscot continues the line of the bookcases' height. One of the original gas-lit wall sconces with a plain square backplate designed by Niedecken is mounted on the pilaster between the areas. A pair of art-glass windows, with a narrow matching panel between, is partially suppressed into the wainscoting. These interior windows, framed by plain moldings, face a service area, not an outside wall.

Figure 158. (opposite)

ENTRY HALL (TOWARD LIBRARY) OF THE MAYER HOUSE.

The stylish Arts and Crafts aesthetic of the house's interiors reflect the versatility and creative talents of George Niedecken. Referencing the exterior style, Tudor Revival and Craftsman-style influences appear throughout the first floor. Niedecken conventionalized motifs from nature into geometric units of abstract ornament for use in the art-glass designs of this home. At the top of the sidelight, a highly stylized bee appears, and a frog is seen below. By the far corner (seen from the outside in Figure 157), both motifs reappear in the library's two front windows and in the front reception room to the right (see Figure 160). Opposite the front door vestibule is a doorway to the dining room. Box beams articulate the various areas of this open space, and align with trim elements on the wall at left that recall half-timbering. Period photographs show the now-open library space was once shielded by a partial-height screen wall that occurred where a partial-height post interrupts the built-in bookcases.

Figure 160.

RECEPTION ROOM OF THE MAYER HOUSE.

Among the best surviving ensembles of his work, this room retains much of Niedecken's original vision for a fully integrated design. Also an accomplished fine artist, Niedecken painted the "Woodland Birches" mural above the fireplace, and it is referenced by the highly figured, curly birch of the room's woodwork. The mural's earthy, autumnal colors were repeated in the room's decorative scheme. The original furniture is now displayed in the Milwaukee Art Museum, but the homeowners opted to have the various pieces reproduced to recreate the original design of the room. So far, the fireplace chairs, a small book table, the floor lamp, the area carpet, and a display cabinet (out of view) have each been precisely recreated. The Roman-brick fireplace's distinctive circular andirons are surviving original elements, which continue the abstracted motifs of nature. The recessed channel of backlit, art-glass panels devised by Niedecken for the ceiling perimeter remains astonishingly contemporary, and unites the overall scheme. The bay window at left is lined by a built-in window seat, and overlooks the open front porch with lake views filtered through trees.

Figure 161.

DINING ROOM (TOWARDS ENTRY HALL) OF THE MAYER HOUSE.

A diagonal view into the entry hall and library beyond is offered through the dining room's main doorway hung with portières (doorway draperies). Inspired by the home's Tudor Revival exterior, Niedecken's design for this room's wood-work is more richly developed than in adjacent areas. The prominent use of art glass is continued, with the upper doors of the built-in sideboard fitted with panels to match the room's windows seen in Figure 162. Aligned with the wain-scoting, the mirror behind the sideboard's niche is high enough to reflect parts of the room. Moldings connected to the ceiling extend the sideboard's vertical proportions. With decoratively cut edges, the horizontal casings above the side-board and doorway are mounted with shallow shelf-like caps resting on small corbels. Matching one in Figure 159, a pair of Niedecken's original gas-lit wall sconces with plain, square backplates flank the sideboard. Narrow original recessed light-ing, running along two sides of the room, is also evident at upper right.

(continued from page 147)

While most Tudor Revival homes display half-timbering somewhere on their exteriors, some examples were built entirely of masonry construction, both of stone and brick. These other variations of English homes are derived from a similar historic period, and closely aligned with the Tudor Revival if not integral to it. One variation broadly referred to as the English Cottage style is further discussed in the second part of this chapter, and is predominantly found in smaller-scale examples. Other English-derived style variations were historically concurrent with the Tudor period, but by their rarified nature had more limited applications, and were generally reserved for much larger-scale, and sometimes palatial, homes, or possibly on apartment houses, or public buildings. The general appearance of these period style homes varies far enough beyond the Tudor Revival style to warrant assigning them separate names.

Most significant among these variations were homes described as in the so-called Elizabethan Revival style, which was applied to homes that specifically adapted the grandly scaled domestic architecture and often, the interior design of the sixteenth century period of the English monarch, Elizabeth I. While still correct to include it under the Tudor umbrella, this particular style reflected trends of its later period,

when an influence of the Italian Renaissance with its attendant classical motifs began to appear in England, and was blended, sometimes boldly, into the more specifically English-born vocabulary of the earlier period. Usually expressed entirely in stone (most often limestone), or sometimes in a combination of stone and red brick, homes that revived this style or its influence in America were first built in the later nineteenth century, sometimes as elegant urban townhouses in large cities, or as imposing country estates in exclusive enclaves or resort areas of the rich. The demand for such displays of extravagance all but vanished after the 1920s, with the onset of the Great Depression.

Another Tudor-related style variation, usually dubbed the Jacobean Revival style, is based on the architectural style of a slightly later period in English history, the late sixteenth and early seventeenth century. It adapts elements of fashionable taste from homes and interiors dating to the time of King James I; most often, this style is expressed in red brick, accented by light-colored stone (usually limestone) detailing (SEE FIGURE 163). Like the Elizabethan Revival style, it appeared in some examples of large-scale homes of the very wealthy. Both of these styles would have required an architect with a particular skill and talent for interpreting historic styles inside and out; of the caliber who worked successfully in the so-called Beaux Arts

(continued on page 159)

Figure 162.

DINING ROOM OF THE MAYER HOUSE.

Viewed through its wide entry doorway and toward the left, most of the dining room's features come into view. The original, narrow recessed lighting channel extends for the room's full length, and repeats on the opposite wall. Woodwork elements include a box-beam ceiling and high wainscot with a plate rail, and panels created by an overlay of shallow moldings below it. The room's focal point is a shallow bay with four art-glass windows; the repeating abstracted form of a bird appears in the glass. The framework of moldings above the bay inventively adapts the half-timbering motifs of the home's façade. In a typically thoughtful Niedecken detail, note how the horizontal line of the double-hung sash on the single window aligns with the wainscoting. While of the same period, the chandelier is not original to the room.

Figure 163.

GLENSHEEN (CONGDON MANSION)
DULUTH, MINNESOTA (1905–08).
Designed by St. Paul architect Clarence H. Johnston and built as the primary residence of Chester A. and Clara Congdon, this palatial home's sloping site fronts directly onto Lake Superior. The extensive grounds were designed by New York Landscape architect Charles W. Leavitt, Jr. With more than 27,000 square feet inside the 39-room house, this grandly scaled estate is in a rare state of preservation. Its original furnishings and finishes are intact, as it stayed in the family until bequeathed to the University of Minnesota-Duluth in 1977. The exterior style can be called Jacobean Revival, as it resembles the grand, domestic architecture of the period of King James I, from early seventeenth-century England. The style is characterized by the use of red brick with pale limestone trim, steeply pitched roofs, and peaked gables without over-hangs. At center are the three tall art glass windows that light the staircase landing seen in Figure 164. The single-story breakfast room in Figure 167 is visible at far right. The Glensheen estate opened to the public as a house museum in 1979.

The Jacobean Revival style adapts elements
of fashionable taste from homes and interiors
dating to the time of King James I.

Figure 164.

MAIN STAIRWAY LANDING DETAIL AT GLENSHEEN.

Located at the mid-floor landing of the main staircase, this stunning set of leaded art-glass windows faces the lake, and can be located in Figure 163. Mostly clear glass was used to maximize daylight and preserve outlooks. Its stylized floral motifs and the composition's sense of geometry suggest British Arts and Crafts sources. In the lower panels, the black and white chequered borders encircling the medallions and central shield recall Vienna Secessionist motifs. Of late medieval English derivation and revived in the Arts and Crafts era, the so-called Tudor rose is repeated throughout. Chicago's Linden Art Glass Company is known to have provided art glass in this house, and also were the makers of art glass for projects of Frank Lloyd Wright. The home's interior design is credited to the William A. French Company of St. Paul, in collabora-tion with important Minneapolis designer John Bradstreet (1845-1914), who was responsible for creating most of the unexpectedly high-style Arts and Crafts room schemes that follow. Most of the primary public rooms in Glensheen that are not included here express more traditional period-style design influences of English derivation.

Figure 165.

RECEPTION ROOM DETAIL AT GLENSHEEN.

Located near the front door, this room was where guests would first be received by family members. As with most other rooms, this retains the original furnishings, fittings, and finishes. While not Arts and Crafts in overall style, the room has aspects of progressive design. Mounted on the underside of the projecting wood cornice around the room's ceiling are small light fixtures with handblown iridescent glass shades, a detail that appears only in this room. Above the lights, the entire coved ceiling is finished in gold leaf. The walls are covered with a delicately hued, silk damask fabric. One of two, the doorway is fitted with pocket doors, and overlaid with lustrous gold portières of hand-stenciled silk velvet. Matching fabric was utilized for the upholstery and window draperies in this room. Originally, the public rooms featured fine Persian and other Oriental carpets, but most are stored for safekeeping or kept, partially rolled, out of the way; the red carpet protects the oak floors during house tours, but compromises the subtly elegant color scheme.

Figure 166.

LIBRARY AT GLENSHEEN.

Adjoining the main living room through a wide doorway opposite the fireplace wall, the library has a cozier feeling, but is much larger than this view suggests. Paneled in deep red mahogany, the room's fireplace alcove is lined with built-in bookcases that repeat around the room. The alcove's fireplace surround of iridescent glass tiles is the room's most arresting feature. With a luminous quality, its delicately gridded pattern surrounds an inset panel of scrolling forms and floral motifs that show an Arts and Crafts influence. To the right, the room expands into a large bay window (seen in Figure 163, to the left of the arched rear entrance), with an inviting, brightly lit sitting area overlooking the lake. Time and daylight have diminished the original rich effect of the fabric-covered walls. The armchair at left retains its distinctive and original Art Nouveau upholstery treatment. The original Oriental rug is partially rolled up, to the right (the blue rug is only for floor protection).

Figure 167.

BREAKFAST ROOM AT GLENSHEEN.

The finest example of Arts and Crafts design in the house, the breakfast room is the work of John Bradstreet. While much of the wall area is windows, the room's floor and remaining wall space are covered in matte-green, glazed Rookwood tile. Reinterpreted by Bradstreet, a traditional Japanese wood-finishing technique, called "jin-di-sugi," was applied to both the custom furniture and woodwork of this room. Generally used on cypress, it involves searing the wood, and scraping it to raise and highlight the grain. Bradstreet repeated this treatment in the smoking room (seen in Figure 168). Stylized oak leaves and acorns enrich the upper reaches of the perimeter art-glass windows. The central copper and glass pendant fixture was produced by the Handicraft Guild of Minneapolis. The butler's pantry and kitchen are to the left, and the outside rear terrace and dining room are to the right.

Figure 168.

SMOKING ROOM DETAIL AT GLENSHEEN.

Another of John Bradstreet's sophisticated Arts and Crafts creations, the smoking room has a decidedly Japanese inspiration. The wood elements of the upper walls and ceiling were given a Japanese finish treatment (see Figure 167). Ceiling beams wrap down the walls at either end, connecting with plain wood trim that outlines a series of horizontal panels and creates a linear frieze. From its lower edge, curvilinear wooden arms extend outward to suspend small copper-shaded lights, which repeat around the room and light artwork. Secured to a wooden block on a ceiling beam, four lights hang low on chains while a fifth remains close to the round copper ceiling backplate. Now tarnished with age, the material between the ceiling beams and the upper walls may have originally had a reflective silver finish. In the manufacture of the lower wall covering, natural-colored grasscloth was applied over a silver-finished paper, which reflects through the woven texture.

Figure 169.

SECOND FLOOR HALLWAY DETAIL AT GLENSHEEN.

This decorative wall treatment of the second floor hall extends from the top of the main stairway in two directions, to the master suite and the daughters' bedrooms. The floral motif of the stenciled borders adapts the Tudor rose in the main stairway landing's art-glass window (seen in Figure 164). With some hand-painted infill, the stenciling shows off skillfully blended colorings and crisp linework in harmony with the oak woodwork. The painted walls have a "Tiffany finish" popular in the Arts and Crafts era. Characterized by a blended application of paint colors (taken from the borders), paint is applied in multiple layers and worked by hand with rags and brushes. The resulting misty, mottled texture has been likened to the blended, matte glazes on the era's art pottery. One of a pair of matching sidelights flanks an art glass–faced door, made by Chicago Linden Art Glass Company, to the master bedroom suite.

Figure 170.

SECOND FLOOR BEDROOM DETAIL AT GLENSHEEN.

Although not hers during childhood, this was the last bedroom occupied by Elisabeth, the youngest daughter, and Glensheen's final Congdon family resident. Its decoration reflects a softer, more feminine taste than in the adjoining hallways seen in Figure 169. The detail shows part of the fireplace and built-in cabinetry. A low-relief carving of the "tree of life" motif on the central cabinet doors shows a distinct Art Nouveau influence. Possibly adapted from the colors in the handblown art-glass shade of the wall sconce, the pale, greenish gray enamel painted finish is original. The exquisitely crafted silver wall sconce, one of two above the fireplace, with other matching fixtures in the room, exhibits the quality of fine jewelry. Recalling the Prairie style, the geometric pattern of the mosaic fireplace surround employs mostly pale colors, a complement to the art-glass light shades. The subtle bamboo-patterned wallpaper, with a matching frieze above the picture rail, was discovered to be the first of multiple layers installed over time in this room, and may possibly be part of the original decorative scheme.

Figure 171.

THIRD FLOOR BEDROOM FIREPLACE AT GLENSHEEN.

With vertical proportions and modest scale, this fireplace has simple detailing expressed in painted wood with squared corbels lined up beneath a high mantel shelf. In classic Arts and Crafts style, the inset Grueby tile panel, comprised of eight separate tiles that create a stylized pine tree landscape, is a signature motif of the company. They also made the rectangular field tiles, matte-glazed in a golden yellow, which face the surrounding area, and are laid in the running bond pattern. The outlines of the fireplace opening and inset panel conform to the field tile's modular size. This room was nicknamed "the infirmary," as it was the preferred place for quiet resting or convalescing from illnesses. Supposedly, the fireplace opening was raised up to enable bedridden occupants across the room to get a better view of it. This and the other third floor bedrooms showcase John Bradstreet's particular skill at interpreting Arts and Crafts design.

Figure 173.

THIRD FLOOR SITTING ROOM AT GLENSHEEN.

This room is between two of the sons' bedrooms, and was planned as an informal, shared space. The upper side walls' angles reflect the forms of the roof gable at the center of the rear elevation seen in Figure 163. Built-in shelves and storage align with the depth of the fireplace, where a surround of handmade blue-green glazed tile incorporates narrow, low-relief borders. The line above the fireplace mantel wall carries around the room, and is aligned with an open shelf above the sofa, to which a pair of reading lights are attached. The room's sturdy, matching furniture by John Bradstreet is finely executed and well proportioned. Except for the rocker, the pieces have ebonized inlaid geometric borders and small medallion accents that suggest a progressive Austrian or German influence. This room's fourth wall is completely open to the adjacent hall-way (seen in Figure 172), and the same crown molding outlining this ceiling continues into the hallway. The painted finish within the wainscot's panels is also repeated there below a simpler chair rail molding (see Figure 172). The original, stenciled decoration is well documented, and will be restored. To avoid excessive wear during tours, the room's original carpet is partially rolled up.

Figure 172.

THIRD FLOOR HALLWAY DETAIL AT GLENSHEEN.

Dedicated to the sons' bedrooms, the third floor is reached from a separate smaller open staircase at one end of the second floor hallway. At each successive floor level, Glensheen's interior decoration becomes less complex. John Bradstreet created the Arts and Crafts decorative scheme, detailing, and furniture designs for each room on this floor. The Arts and Crafts tendency toward simpler forms, earthy colors, and lack of pretension made it a logical choice for the boys' territory. The simplicity of the woodwork detailing looks plain in comparison to that of other floors, and indicates a Craftsman-style influence. Bradstreet's awareness of progressive international design may have influenced the repeating geometric designs of the stenciled borders at the top of the walls, whose stylized motifs are adapted from plant forms that recall European Arts and Crafts examples. The soft textures and warm colors of the painted walls are in harmony with the woodwork. The simple, square gas-lit wall sconce appears repeatedly on this level.

(Continued from page 151)

style, generally associated with monumental public buildings, and private homes of corresponding extravagance. Beaux Arts influences were typically derived from Classical or Renaissance sources, but were also known to tap into various other grand historic styles such as Gothic, Elizabethan, or Jacobean Revival upon client request. In the eclectic mode of the 1920s, some examples employed distinct combinations of those two alternative English styles into one, humorously nicknamed "Jacobethan." Even more eclectic design variations of this might also introduce half-timbering effects into the mix.

For new home budgets that could afford it, approximating the "neo-medieval" taste of Morris by the 1920s was relatively easy and almost formulaic for architects and interior designers. The use of wallpapers and fabrics then still made by Morris and Co. was among the easiest paths in this direction. An example of greater commitment to English Arts and Crafts was the use of richly colored, leaded art glass accents applied to windows both large and small. More often, plain diamond-patterned leading set into casement-style windows would at least suffice for an authentic Tudor reference. In terms of furnishings, a mixture of English antiques if they could be afforded, along with some suitably styled new furniture, was considered most desirable and often depicted in home design-advice books and periodicals. Lighting fixtures in Tudor Revival—style homes could range from Gothic-style spiky shapes in iron, to tamer models usually of brass, borrowed from later English periods. Such eclecticism in lighting design was to be expected. Another expressive and versatile element to introduce was a flattened arch called a Tudor arch, which could be applied to the tops of windows and doors, as well as to the designs of paneling, built-in cabinetry, fireplace openings, and mantels. At least in the living room, mantels of carved wood or stone (sometimes of cast stone) were typical features. During the 1920s, Tudor Revival chimneys, in tall, tapering hooded forms, often extended to the ceiling. Other places to make overtly English references influence included "Gothicized" beamwork, especially when set into peaked living room ceilings, decorative carving of wood paneling such as the period-correct "linenfold" style (SEE FIGURE 177), as well as carved brackets, corbels, and rail spindles (SEE FIGURES 176 AND 178). Usually reserved for a grander home's public rooms, the art of ornamental plasterwork was a Tudor tradition, and an active part of its revival. Some of it was quite restrained and of rather low relief, but the most elaborate examples might incorporate striking Gothic-style rib-vaults, or the swooping, flattened curves of Tudor-inspired "strapwork."

Despite America's ongoing fixation with emulating the styles imported from England starting from our Colonial period onward, the resulting examples somehow tended to be recognizably different than the original models, even though they faithfully incorporated their elements. With each successive style, America seemed to grow more confident in its ability to "improve" what England gave us, and our adaptations grew markedly freer. Following in the tradition and spirit of independence which has guided America, we have somehow managed to make these "imported styles" all our own.

Figure 174.

THIRD FLOOR BEDROOM
AT GLENSHEEN.

This was Edward Congdon's bedroom. As the second oldest son, he was almost an adult when the house was finally finished. The angled ceiling configuration in the corner reflects the intersection of this room's rear facing dormer roof, and that of the main roof, which runs the length of the house at a right angle from the dormer. In this bedroom, and in another very similar one on the other side of the sitting room through the door at right, Bradstreet devised some practical built-ins below these angles to utilize the oddly shaped, leftover space. At right is a small fireplace faced in deep green tiles that is fitted with a handcrafted copper hood in the Craftsman style. Above the mantel is a pair of matching copper sconces. Custom designed for the room by John Bradstreet, the furniture is a more refined variation of the Craftsman style. Surviving textiles original to this room include the small carpet under the writing table, as well as the table runner and the bed spread, which each have appliquéd Arts and Crafts motif. This room's missing original stenciled decoration will eventually be restored.

English Cottage Style

The early twentieth century interpretations of the English Cottage style include a range of examples so broadly interpreted that establishing consistently specific characteristics for its definition is an elusive task. Almost more of an attitude of architectural posturing than a true style, it was used as a formulaic recipe for an appealingly packaged American home. At first, public perception of exactly what constituted an English Cottage had a parallel in the occasional but persistent confusion over what really defined a bungalow. The English Cottage was associated with being a style of smaller, modest homes by some, and by others as simply another historic revival style to be applied to homes of any size. Despite the existence of many larger-scale examples that would seem to refute the first opinion, the housing type most often associated with the English Cottage style was indeed the bungalow.

Although created by many of the same influences that originally spawned the Tudor Revival style, the English Cottage style emerged slightly later, and didn't become a major housing style quite as quickly. In the context of the American Arts and Crafts movement, perhaps the earliest and most high-profile place where a pronounced English influence was apparent was in Elbert Hubbard's famous Roycroft Community in East Aurora, New York; it was founded in 1895, after Hubbard had made an inspiring trip to England the previous year. For the campus of the Roycrofters, Hubbard envisioned the buildings in styles directly inspired by those he had seen in England. Most of the campus buildings reflect an English Tudor influence, and feature an extensive use of half-timbering and stone. The 1902 former Roycroft Blacksmith Shop is a stone-walled English Cottage—style structure with Tudor-inspired half-timbering in its upper gables, and roofing of handmade terra cotta tiles such as those used on many historic English structures of the Tudor period. Years later, Hubbard's son Bert would continue the Roycroft tradition of English influence on his own Tudor Revival home (SEE FIGURES 175–178).

Two other important American Arts and Crafts communities reflected an English influence in their architecture, and members of the same group of like-minded associates from Philadelphia founded both. The leading personality for these efforts was architect William Lightfoot Price (1861–1916), who was most experienced at designing homes for a wealthy clientele. Conceived as "utopian" crafts communities (and like the Roycroft and Byrdcliffe communities, patterned after similar English examples), they became known for handcrafted furniture, pottery, and bookbindings. Founded in 1901, Rose Valley is situated close to Philadelphia, and its buildings reflect a blended Arts and Crafts sensibility with both Tudor Revival and English Cottage inspiration. Surviving only until 1906, it had limited commercial success. The other crafts community was called Arden, founded about the same time, not far from Rose Valley, but in Delaware, outside of Wilmington. Arden's architecture is generally simpler and more modestly scaled, but its homes by Will Price shared similar influences with those at Rose Valley, although more from the Craftsman style and bungalows is apparent there. Rose Valley survives mostly as an enclave of original homes by Price and his collaborators; Arden has since evolved into a latter-day version of a crafts community. Both historically significant sites are possible to explore today.

During the ensuing popularity of the Craftsman style, the concept if not the precise image, of an English Cottage was considered a suitable inspiration for

Figure 175.

HUBBARD HILL, EAST AURORA, NEW YORK (1929).

This grand, Tudor Revival—style home was built by Elbert Hubbard II, the son of Roycroft founder Elbert Hubbard, as his own residence. Nicknamed "Bert," he had taken over the business of the Roycroft community after his father and stepmother died in the 1915 sinking of the Lusitania. It is one of the area's most imposing residences and is sited on a hill above East Aurora. Bert utilized Roycroft artisans to complete the interior finish work, which included handcrafted metalwork for its hardware and lighting fixtures, and skillfully hand-carved, wooden details. Much wider than its depth, Hubbard Hill was designed as a rambling, horizontal composition, which on approach makes it seem even more imposing. The house was deliberately designed to appear as if it had been added to over a long period of time, suggested by the shifts in materials and detailing that occur across the front. At the center of the half-timbered area is a recessed front door, and the service wing is at left. Containing a spiral staircase, the circular tower with a conical roof is a form more associated with French Gothic than English Tudor buildings. The main living room is on the far right side with the chimney.

Figure 176.

LIVING ROOM DETAIL AT HUBBARD HILL.

Modeled after the great halls of Tudor-era manor houses, the living room is spanned by several wooden trusses that support its steeply peaked ceiling. These are embellished with details, handcarved by Roycroft artisans, that adapt Gothic forms. A series of smaller crossing beams divides the ceiling spaces between them. Draped with a collection of Japanese "obis," a second floor "minstrel's gallery" (balcony) overlooking the room has a turned-spindle railing. Behind its door, with a flattened "Tudor arch," is one end of the second floor hallway. Underneath the balcony, a larger doorway of similar form and with handcarved detailing, adjoins a smaller arched opening fitted with a spindled screen. On the other side of these is the entry hall. From there, the tower staircase and front door are both to the left.

Figure 177.

DINING ROOM WALL DETAIL AT HUBBARD HILL.

With a lower ceiling than the living room and a more intimate feeling, the dining room adjoins the entry hall through this pair of Tudor arch double doors, which are each divided by pairs of small recessed panels. Above the doors are panels with deeply hand-carved motifs of sinuous vines and leaves. Occurring only on one wall of the room, paneling extends from floor to ceiling, and displays the so-called "linenfold" pattern in its panelized squares. Also the carving work of Roycroft artisans, this is a characteristic English motif of the Tudor period that was applied to both architecture and furniture. The linenfold name references the undulating motif, seen in each of the square panels, that adapts the forms of folded or draped fabric.

Figure 178.

BREAKFAST ROOM AT HUBBARD HILL.

Lit by the morning sun, the breakfast room is divided from one end of the dining room by an open colonnade, and may be screened off by draperies. With an English Arts and Crafts aesthetic, the colonnade's construction details reflect traditional joinery techniques, with the tops of each curved corbel notched into the lintel beam above. To either side are low railings with turned spindles. Down a step, the slate floor is a practical choice, as this room has direct access, through the arch-topped door, to a small exterior terrace leading to the lawn and garden areas. Above the door, a carved panel adapts forms of Gothic-style tracery in high relief. Used here for decoration, a traditional Japanese cooking device suspended from a beam on a bamboo pole was contrived for heating an iron kettle over hot coals in a metal-lined wooden box (brazier). A whimsical fish form crafted in metal is incorporated into its otherwise utilitarian design.

bungalows. For example, Gustav Stickley's interest in applying some English influence to his own Craftsman home designs, typically, a simple interpretation of half-timbering, was also extended to smaller-scale bungalow plans. As a popular tastemaker, Stickley's stamp of approval had considerable weight, and his sanctioning of English-derived influences in his house plans and articles in the *Craftsman* magazine convinced many of their suitability as crossover companions to otherwise Craftsman-style homes.

In addition to those from Stickley, selections in plan books began to feature more home designs likened to English Cottages, although there was inconsistency in how that association was justified during the Craftsman heyday. But by the 1920s, it was apparent that the Craftsman style wasn't holding up to the test of time or fashion that Stickley had hoped, and the public had developed a growing appetite for more variety and novelty in their choices for plan book home design and decoration (SEE FIGURE 179). In the so-called English Cottage, the home-building business found a style with an infectious appeal. Moreover, it handily crossed over from small planning formats to larger ones.

But what were the essential ingredients of this style that seemed to captivate so many? Probably the general characteristic most widely agreed upon was that the demeanor of an English Cottage–style home should have or at least suggest the posture of modesty, as evoked by the term "cottage," coupled with some degree of recognizably English character. From there, a more precise definition still remains debatable. With the presence of some defining features, it seems a rather wide variety of homes, regardless of their size, may be described as English Cottage style.

The architectural feature most consistently linked to the English Cottage style is the form of its roof. One that is commonly associated with this style emulates the appearance of a thatched roof, a feature common to many historic dwellings of varying sizes in the English countryside. Slate roofs are also linked to this style, and tend to appear on homes with very shallow eaves. They were historically most compatible with masonry-built cottages of stone such as in England's Cotswolds Region. The weight of slate roofs made them less practical or appropriate for Craftsman-style roofs with deeply overhanging eaves, but they were compatible on crossover Craftsman homes with a Tudor Revival style influence. Often variegated in color and texture, slate remains the most elegant and refined (and expensive) roofing treatment for most homes of both the Tudor Revival and English Cottage styles.

Fired clay (terra-cotta) roofing tiles were also utilized on historic English Cottages as well as on many other buildings. More likely to be found in areas that had

Figure 180.

HOUSE IN AMHERST, NEW YORK (CA. 1925).

While the mock-thatched roof is a compelling feature of this English Cottage–style house, the masonry treatment of its exterior walls is the real standout. Irregularly sized blocks of stone have been laid so that some project further than others. Above each of the variously sized arched and squared openings, the direction shift in the stones' placement gives emphasis to the symmetrically composed façade. The stones' perceived depth around these openings creates the impression of thick walls, further suggested by the recessed front door. A variation of the hipped form, the roof has a low, wide central attic dormer. The rolled eaves extend to the tops of the second floor windows at the center, giving the house a low-slung impression, reinforced by the roof's dramatic slope to the first level on either side. On the right, the roof shelters an inviting, open covered porch that is buffered by carefully composed landscaping. On the left side, the covered space is glass-enclosed.

Figure 179.

DESIGN FOR A HOUSE (1926).

Called "The Honor," this home was listed in Sears, Roebuck and Company's ready-cut plan book Honor Built Modern Homes *for $3,278. Colonial Revival influence is apparent in the symmetry of the front façade, and in the detailing of its small covered entry porch (portico). With a shallow, hipped roof supported by a pair of classical columns, and matching pilasters by its front door, the porch adjoins low concrete terraces ringed by flower boxes. Wall-mounted trellises add interest to either side. The rectangular, two-story form has few distinctive details other than its "mock-thatched" roof, where gentle swells in the roofing material occur above three pairs of bedroom windows. Although only wood shingles were specified for this exterior, a narrow line of molding aligned with the second floor windowsills encircles the entire house, suggesting a potential shift in color (or material) at that point. In plan, the house is entered directly into the living room.*

Figure 181.

HOUSE IN AMHERST, NEW YORK (CA. 1925).

This English Cottage–style house features mock-thatching on both first and second floor roof areas. Asymmetrically composed, the home is entered from the right side, and a wide bay projecting from its center defines its front façade. This allows the primary roof, a variation of the hipped form, to extend forward over the bay and pull down tightly over the second floor windows like the brim of a hat. On either side, the rolled roof flares out, before retreating back to the prevailing level of the other eaves. The first floor's brick walls extend upward, almost to the second floor windowsills. Overhangs with mock-shingled second floor walls are flared outward, just above the brick, which complements the curving roofline. Grouped multi-paned casement windows minimize openings and simplify the façade.

Figure 182.

HOUSE IN BRIGHTON, NEW YORK (CA. 1925).

Prominent Syracuse architect Ward Wellington Ward (1870-1932) designed this unique interpretation of the English Cottage style in this community near Rochester. Ward is well known for his skill at adapting English styles in unusual, inventive ways. The rectangular, two-and-a-half story home, with wood-shingled, mock-thatch roof treatment, is configured with two large side-facing gables. Mostly vertical simple half-timbering is arranged to integrate the windows. On the second floor façade, two matching window pairs have arching tops, with corresponding curves in the roofing above them. The first floor grouping of four windows lends horizontality and balance. Most of the windows feature diamond-paned divisions. In the most exceptional feature, a third of the roof's width is extended, forward and down, from the top of the second floor. Halfway, it sprouts a small arch-topped dormer, with a flower box. Sloping to an almost improbably low level, it shelters the front door, within a modest entry porch largely screened by mature evergreen plantings.

less plentiful supplies of slate, such tile was almost as durable, and had an attractive effect. Sometimes roof tiles had shapes that resembled cut wood shingles, with rounded ends. The tiles were hung in overlapping rows much like wooden shingles, on nails driven into the roof's wood framing. Sometimes this kind of tiling was also employed as a durable exterior wall finish. For more of a snug fit, other roof tiles were formed into interlocking shapes.

Separate from the issue of its construction materials, creating the look or at least the feeling of an English Cottage roof could be achieved in a variety of ways. Usually the least expensive way was to construct the roof with proportions that conveyed the desired "cottagey" feeling by implication, rather than by trying to replicate historic examples. One way this could be done was to reduce the roof's apparent bulk or mass by diagonally clipping the peaks off their gable ends, creating what is called a "jerkin-headed" gable (SEE FIGURE 183). This particular roof configuration has long been a traditional European construction detail, and was indeed employed for many actual English cottages with either slate, tile, or thatched roofs, as well as in larger homes and even some public buildings in England and the rest of Europe. Like half-timbering, this detail had already shown up in the complex roof structures of some homes in America's Queen Anne style, where it was less obvious as an English Cottage reference. On simpler homes, such clipped gables tend to make them seem a bit lower than they really are, and, especially on bungalows, also give the impression of a smaller overall appearance. These qualities fed handily into the popularly perceived image of an English Cottage, and clipped gables became a very popular roof detail, especially in the 1920s.

Among the most technically difficult and more expensive of English Cottage style roof treatments were those that opted to simulate thatching, for an actual thatched roof was considered too impractical for most to ever consider. Despite their cost, mock thatch roofs were applied to both small and large homes (SEE FIGURES 179–182 AND 186). To achieve or suggest this effect, most builders employed irregularly cut, wooden shingles, and it was necessary for many of these to be steam-bent. Applied in wavy, undulating courses of slightly varying widths, they also had to conform to the downwardly curving line of the roof's eaves. To achieve the rolled edge effect, the shingles were laid over a specially made wooden substructure to ensure that the roof's rounded appearance and thickness would approximate that of a thatched roof. Such examples could vary considerably in their finish and quality as well as their aesthetic success; some less expensive and usually less successful attempts at the thatched effect used ordinary composition shingles instead of wooden ones. Many mock-thatch roofs have suffered from chronic neglect, or subsequent applications of inappropriate composition shingling over the original wood. For many, such roofs have retained their English Cottage charm, but they have also proven to be one of the most expensive of all roofs to repair or replace.

Not usually associated with that firm's work, Greene and Greene's design for a Northern California country house incorporated a mock-thatch roof. Called Green Gables, the Woodside, California, estate home was built in 1914 for the Fleishhacker family. In response to a specific request by the clients, Charles Green was entirely responsible for its design. although it was still a project of the firm. The Fleishhackers were pointedly more interested in the English Cottage style than in the high-end Craftsman style mode most associated with the firm's work, and they got their wish. It

> Compared to Tudor Revival, the English Cottage style comes across as friendlier, for it tends to project a more outwardly welcoming aura through its informality.

Figure 183.

SOUTH FRONT OF "BEAUPORT" (SLEEPER-McCANN HOUSE), GLOUCESTER, MASSACHUSETTS (1907–34).

Built as a summer home by Boston interior designer and collector Henry Davis Sleeper (1878-1934), "Beauport" is an intensely personal statement. On a neck of land called Eastern Point, facing Gloucester Harbor, the property is at the edge of a granite cliff. Sleeper's acquisition of period paneling from a dilapidated eighteenth-century home prompted Beauport's initial construction. Starting out as a modest cottage, Beauport evolved into this rambling structure, under the ongoing guidance of local architect Halfdan M. Hanson. English Arts and Crafts influence is seen in Gothic-inspired detailing of wood, brick, and stone. The attached tower at right houses an intimate two story library, and was added in 1911. Despite its exterior's unusual charm, Beauport is most significant for its interiors. After visiting Virginia's historic sites, Sleeper's taste shifted toward Colonial Americana. After his death, Charles E. F. and Helena McCann bought the house and contents and changed few features. In 1942, Beauport became a house museum, open to the public.

Figure 184.

EAST FRONT OF BEAUPORT.

Hidden from the street by a high brick wall, it is difficult to capture Beauport's rambling form in a single photograph. A small open porch framed by a gothic arch marks the front door. To the right, on the second floor, a small balcony locates Sleeper's bedroom. The library tower is partially seen at far left. Housed within the largest forward-facing gable is a two-story space that began as a medieval-inspired hall. Following the 1923 installation of rare, eighteenth-century Chinese wallpaper, it became the China Trade Room. The belfry cupola tops an irregularly massed wing that includes a secondary staircase in its curving stone end. To far right, the roof of the Pembroke Room (or Pine Kitchen) is partly visible. Begun in 1917, it is Sleeper's recreation of a Colonial-era kitchen and as among the largest rooms in the house, it was a favorite place for him to entertain. His circle of well-connected friends included the renowned art collector Isabella Stewart Gardner, whose palatial Boston home, Fenway Court, is now the Gardner Museum. Sleeper's friend and client, Henry Francis duPont, was so impressed with the Pembroke Room that it helped inspire him to shift his collecting focus from European to American antiques. This would lead to the eventual conversion of duPont's family home into Winterthur Museum, a famous repository of American decorative art, (named after its Delaware location).

Figure 185.

HOUSE IN BRIGHTON, NEW YORK (CA. 1925).

Larger than it looks, the irregular composition of this picturesque home near Rochester keeps its streetside profile low. Of stone and brick, with a slate roof, it adapts a variation of the English Cottage style, and is another example of a design composed as if it had been built in different phases. The two front-facing gables, with no overhang, extend below the level of the second floor. Some brick is introduced in the towering chimney tops, and in a decorative attic-level vent in the largest gable at center. The random, rough-textured stone walls are a unifying device. In pleasing contrast to the stone are a few smooth, pale limestone accents. This house takes some of its inspiration from the stone cottage vernacular style of England's Cotswolds region. During the later English Arts and Crafts period, important designer C.R. Ashbee (1863-1942) relocated his Guild of Handicraft from London to the rural Cotswolds village of Chipping Campden in 1902, where it flourished for only a few years. An important example of a "utopian" Arts and Crafts community, this working model was adapted, in both Europe and America, for similar craft ventures.

Figure 186.

HOUSE IN OXNARD, CALIFORNIA (1915).

Although it is quite large, and has some half-timbering details in it gables, this shingled house evokes more of an English Cottage than Tudor Revival feeling. Blended elements of the Craftsman style are seen on the windows and the brackets supporting the gable eaves. Such expansive front porches are generally uncommon on Tudor Revival or English Cottage style homes. Thick, square, ivy-clad columns supporting the porch roof reinforce the Craftsman impression. The use of a single-story gable at the porch entry helps reduce the scale of the house. A more subtle variation of the usual "mock-thatch" effect, the original surviving wood-shingled roof is more gently rounded at the eaves than most examples that attempt this reference. Above the porch entry, the arch across the bottom of the small gable quietly complements the soft curves of the roofline's eaves.

Figure 187.

ENTRY HALL (TOWARD DINING ROOM) OF THE OXNARD HOUSE.

Once inside the house, the Craftsman style takes over. Textured grasscloth wallcovering (also used on the ceiling) complements the warm wood tones. Circulation spaces here are extra-roomy, and openness between public rooms enhances the spacious feeling. Entered from the front door to the right, the entry hall is open in three directions to adjoining spaces. The rear stair hall is opposite the front door, and a slender round newel post is an unexpected detail. Squared spindles on the stair railing are the only painted wood elements in the vicinity. Framed original blueprints for the house are arranged up the side of the stairs. Admitting more light from the stair hall, the horizontal opening in the wall at left is an original feature, and its proportions recall the Prairie style. The dining room doorway at right is fitted with pocket doors. A built-in sideboard extends beneath a pair of casement windows. Set on the high plate rail that encircles the dining room is an unusual series of vintage painted wooden cutout silhouettes, depicting various cowboy scenes, that make an effective variation on the popular period motif of a "landscape frieze."

Figure 188.

HOUSE IN SPOKANE, WASHINGTON (1914).

A more unusual example of Craftsman-style elements assembled with an English Cottage character, this South Hill house has an unassuming yet gracious quality. It was designed by local architect F.D. Hughes for the Murgittroyd family. A circular driveway passes close to the front entry. Instead of a front porch, a modest overhang that characterizes many English-influenced homes shelters the front door. In an otherwise largely symmetrical design, the front door is set off-center to the left, which lends the house a less formal demeanor. Festooned with climbing vines, the warm red brick exterior is subtly detailed, with vertically stacked borders set into its overall "running bond" pattern that are used on the front façade to link the first and second floor windows. The fascia boards (bargeboards) of only the front gables are embellished with some decorative carving. Craftsman-style elements include the brackets under the eaves, and the shed-roof dormer between the two front gables.

is notable that Charles Greene's wife, Alice, was English, and he developed a further affinity to England during extended stays there with his family. Of note is a much earlier example of English influence appearing in the firm's work, the striking 1905 Robinson House in Pasadena, California, where some half-timbering appears on the second floor.

The use of variously shaped dormers is a fairly consistent element in English Cottage–style designs. Because these bring light and additional headroom to attic-level spaces, they tend to appear more prominently on smaller homes with oversized roofs such as on many bungalows; they also appear on two-story homes. Dormers add considerable interest to the rooflines of houses with mock-thatch roofs. On some larger two-story versions, corresponding swellings in the rounded roofing material are aligned above the second floor windows' placement, and lend a sense of movement to the roof's curving form (SEE FIGURES 179 AND 182). So-called "eyebrow" dormers can fit easily into the horizontal curves of mock-thatch roofs, but these can also appear on other types, including conventionally shingled, slate, or clay-tiled roofs.

The storybook appeal of historic examples of European buildings with thatched roofs or half-timbering glimpsed during travels, or in books and periodicals, held great novelty for the American public, making it easy for both styles to be exploited for the housing market. Another distinct influence, which became a potent force in the marketing of fantasy of all kinds to the American public, was the rapidly developing Hollywood movie industry. In set designs, it was not unusual to glimpse buildings that

looked much like English Cottages among the scenes used for historical dramas. The movie industry had a profound effect on public taste, and often, what people saw in films became what they wanted at home.

Compared to Tudor Revival, the English Cottage–style comes across as friendlier, for it tends to project a more outwardly welcoming aura through its informality. This appeal can be further reinforced by pairing such a house with a cottage garden, an old English tradition in which the front yards of rural cottages were treated as living welcome mats for visitors. Lovingly planted and tended, old species of favorite native plants were often preserved there, among a colorful tapestry of other blooming annuals, perennials, flowering shrubs, vines, bulbs, and herbs. These gardens could include plantings of edibles such as berries, vegetables, and fruit trees. Still appealing today is the old cottage garden tradition of sharing and exchanging favorite plant cuttings with visiting friends and neighbors.

Some architects chose to include some half-timbering, the defining feature of the Tudor Revival style, in otherwise mostly English Cottage–style hybrid home designs. Despite this, the appearance of half-timbering still makes a convenient if somewhat fluid dividing line between these styles, especially when deciding what to call them. Despite the fact that the Tudor Revival style was more often applied to larger homes, and the English Cottage style to smaller-scale ones, this chapter's examples show how, without sacrificing a bit of aesthetic appeal, these ratios could be easily reversed.

Figure 189.

LIBRARY OF THE SPOKANE HOUSE.

This cozy retreat is in the front left corner of the house, adjacent to the entry hall. The fireplace features a striking handmade blue-green tile surround, and a decorative inset panel with a stylized peacock motif. Paneled in mahogany, the woodwork is handsomely detailed, and incorporates built-in bookcases to either side of the desk at left. Above the fireplace mantel, the wall is paneled with a series of "ogee" (double-curved) arches, a graceful variation of more typically pointed Gothic arches. The same motif is also adapted at the top and sides of the bookcases. Above the paneling, a recently added deeply colored, paisley-patterned frieze encircles the room. Arts and Crafts period accessories include two small Heinz lamps, Rookwood bookends on the mantel, and an unusual back-painted mica and copper shade used on the lamp at right.

Figure 190.

SUN ROOM OF THE SPOKANE HOUSE.

Adjoining the living room, this cheerful sunroom at the back of the house overlooks the city. It also connects to the dining room through another set of doors out of view. With separate upper panels divided by leaded glass grids, the French doors are distinctively detailed. A series of low radiators are concealed behind wooden grills fitted under the built-in shelf along the windows at right. The fireplace is an unusual feature for a sunroom, but it makes this space particularly appealing. Applied to both the fireplace surround and the floor, a stylish, original, handmade tile treatment utilizes black-glazed field tiles as a foil for amber-colored borders. Coordinating decorative tiles, some enriched with stylized motifs, are accented with a denim blue glaze. The wall treatment above the mantel recalls the intricate geometry of Chinese fretwork, which is complemented by the original Oriental lantern-style fixture. At the center is a rare period "Ali Baba" bench from Roycroft that serves as a coffee table.

RESOURCES

BIBLIOGRAPHY

Anderson, Timothy J.; Eudora M. Moore, and Robert W. Winter (eds.) *California Design 1910*. Pasadena, California: California Design Publications, 1974. Reprint, Santa Barbara, California, and Salt Lake City, Utah: Peregrine Smith, Inc., 1980.

Axelrod, Alan (ed.). *The Colonial Revival in America.* New York, New York, and London, England: W. W. Norton & Company, 1985.

Boutelle, Sara Holmes. *Julia Morgan, Architect.* New York: Abbbeville Press. 1995

Brooks, H. Allen. *Frank Lloyd Wright and the Prairie School.* New York: George Braziller, Inc., in association with Cooper-Hewitt Museum, 1984.

Cathers, David. *Gustav Stickley.* New York: Phaidon Press, Inc., 2003.

Clark, Robert Judson (ed.). *The Arts and Crafts Movement in America.* Princeton, New Jersey: Princeton University Press, 1972.

Crump, James. *F. Holland Day: Suffering the Ideal.* Santa Fe, New Mexico: Twin Palms Publishers, 1995.

Cummings, Kathleen Ann. *Pleasant Home: A History of the John Farson House, George Washington Maher, Architect.* Oak Park, Illinois: The Pleasant Home Foundation, 2002.

Curtis, Nancy, and Richard Nylander et al. *Beauport: The Sleeper-McCann House.* Boston, Massachusetts: Society for the Preservation of New England Antiquities, 1990.

Fleming, John, and Nikolaus Pevsner. *The Penguin Dictionary of Architecture.* Harmondsworth, Middlesex, England: Penguin Books Ltd., 1979.

Freudenheim, Leslie Mandelson, and Elisabeth Sussman. *Building with Nature: Roots of the San Francisco Bay Region Tradition.* Santa Barbara, California, and Salt Lake City, Utah: Peregrine Smith, Inc., 1974.

Gebhard, David, and Robert Winter. *Los Angeles: An Architectural Guide.* Layton, Utah: Gibbs Smith / Peregrine Smith Books, 1994.

Gebhard, David, Eric Sandweiss, and Robert Winter. *The Guide to Architecture in San Francisco and Northern California.* Layton, Utah: Gibbs Smith / Peregrine Smith Books, 1985.

Gebhard, David, and Tom Martinson. *A Guide to the Architecture of Minnesota.* Minneapolis, Minnesota: University of Minnesota Press, 1977.

Goff, Lee. *Tudor Style: Tudor Revival Houses in America from 1890 to the Present.* New York: Universe Publishing, 2002.

Gordon-Van Tine Company. *117 House Designs of the Twenties.* Davenport, Iowa: Gordon-Van Tine Company, 1923. Reprint, Mineola, New York: The Atheneum of Philadelphia and Dover Publications, Inc., 1992.

Green, Nancy E. (ed). *Byrdcliffe: An American Arts and Crafts Colony.* Ithaca, New York: Herbert F. Johnson Museum of Art, 2004.

Hawkins, William J., and William F. Willingham. *Classic Houses of Portland, Oregon 1850-1950.* Portland, Oregon: Timber Press, 1999.

Jones, Robert T. (ed.). *Authentic Small Houses of the Twenties.* New York: Harper and Brothers Publishers, 1929. Reprint, New York: Dover Publications, Inc., 1987.

Kaplan, Wendy. *"The Art That Is Life": The Arts and Crafts Movement in America, 1875-1920.* Boston, Massachussets: Little, Brown and Company, 1987.

Keeler, Charles Augustus. *The Simple Home.* San Francisco, California: P. Elder, 1904. Reprint, Santa Barbara, California, and Salt Lake City, Utah: Peregrine Smith, Inc., 1979.

Kennedy, Roger G. *Mission: The History and Architecture of the Missions of North America.* New York: Houghton Mifflin Company, 1993.

Lancaster, Clay. *The American Bungalow.* New York: Abbeville Press, 1985.

Loizeaux, J. D. *Classic Houses of the Twenties.* Elizabeth, New Jersey: J. D. Loizeaux Lumber Company and the Loizeaux Builders Supply Co., 1927. Reprint, Mineola, New York: The Atheneum of Philadelphia and Dover Publications, Inc., 1992.

Massey, James, and Shirley Maxwell. *Arts & Crafts Design in America: A State-By-State Guide.* San Francisco, California: Chronicle Books, 1998.

McAlester, Virginia and Lee McAlester. *A Field Guide to America's Neighborhoods and Museum Houses: The Western States.* New York: Alfred A. Knopf, 1998.

McCoy, Esther. *Five California Architects.* New York: Praeger Publishers, Inc., 1975.

Naylor, Gillian. *The Arts and Crafts Movement.* London: Studio Vista, 1971.

Olivarez, Jennifer Komar. *Progressive Design in the Midwest: The Purcell-Cutts House and the Prairie School Collection at the Minneapolis Institute of Arts.* Minneapolis, Minnesota: The University of Minnesota Press, 2000.

Parry, Linda (ed.). *William Morris.* London, England: Philip Wilson Publishers Limited, 1996. Reprint, New York: Harry N. Abrams, Inc., 1996.

Peisch, Mark L. *The Chicago School of Architecture.* New York: Random House, 1964.

Robertson, Cheryl. *Frank Lloyd Wright and George Mann Niedecken: Prairie School Collaborators.* Lexington, Massachusetts: Milwaukee Art Museum and Museum of Our National Heritage, 1999.

Sanford, Trent Elwood. *The Architecture of the Southwest.* New York: W. W. Norton Company, Inc. Reprint, Tucson, Arizona: The University of Arizona Press, 1950.

Saylor, Henry H. *Bungalows.* New York: Robert M. McBride and Co., 1911.

Scully, Vincent Jr. *Frank Lloyd Wright.* New York: George Braziller, Inc., 1960.

Scully, Vincent. *The Shingle Style Today.* New York: George Braziller, Inc., 1974.

Sears, Roebuck and Company. *Sears, Roebuck Catalog of Houses, 1926.* Chicago, Illinois, and Philadelphia, Pennsylvania: Sears, Roebuck and Company, 1926. Reprint, New York: The Atheneum of Philadelphia and Dover Publications, Inc., 1991.

Secrest, Meryle. *Frank Lloyd Wright.* New York: Alfred A. Knopf, 1992.

Shoppell, R. W., et al. *Turn of the Century Houses, Cottages, and Villas.* Reprint, Mineola, New York. Dover Publications, 1984.

Smith, Henry Atterbury. *Books of a Thousand Homes, Volume I.* New York: Home Owners Service Bureau, 1923. Reprint, Mineola, New York: Dover Publications, Inc., 1990.

Stickley, Gustav. *The Best of Craftsman Homes.* Santa Barbara, California, and Salt Lake City, Utah: Peregrine Smith, Inc., 1979. (Includes plans from *Stickley's Craftsman Homes* (1909) and *More Craftsman Homes* (1912).)

_____. *Craftsman Bungalows: 59 Homes from "The Craftsman."* Mineola, New York: Dover Publications, Inc., 1988. (Reprint of thirty-six articles selected from issues of *Craftsman* magazine published between December 1903 and August 1916.)

Storrer, William Allin. *The Frank Lloyd Wright Companion.* Chicago: The University of Chicago Press, 1993.

Sutro, Dirk. *San Diego Architecture.* San Diego: San Diego Architectural Foundation, 2002.

Trapp, Kenneth R. (ed.). *The Arts and Crafts Movement in California: Living the Good Life.* New York: Abbeville Press Publishers, 1993.

Von Holst, Hermann Valentin. *Country and Suburban Homes of the Prairie Period.* (Originally published: *Modern American Homes.* Chicago: American Technical Society, 1913.) Reprint, New York: Dover Publications, Inc., 1982.

Wilson, Henry L. *California Bungalows of the Twenties.* Los Angeles, California, Henry L. Wilson, (n.d.). Reprint, Mineola, New York: Dover Publications, Inc., 1993.

Wilson, Richard Guy. *The Colonial Revival House.* New York: Harry N. Abrams, Inc., 2004.

Winter, Robert. *The California Bungalow.* Los Angeles, California: Hennessey & Ingalls, Inc., 1980.

_____. *Craftsman Style.* New York: Harry N. Abrams, Inc., 2004.

Woodbridge, Sally (ed.). *Bay Area Houses: New Edition.* Layton, Utah: Gibbs M. Smith, Inc., 1988.

Resources and How to Use Them

There is an ever-increasing range of architects, design-ers, artisans, craftspeople, workshops, and larger man-ufacturers who offer services or products with an Arts and Crafts sensibility. Many of them offer their services nationally or sell their wares by mail order. Others operate on a smaller scale and prefer working on a local level.

Rather than attempt to assemble a definitive list of every noteworthy resource available today, we have instead opted to include a listing of those current peri-odicals that feature either consistent or occasional cov-erage of Arts and Crafts-related design. Readers will find that most Arts and Crafts-related businesses that sell their services or wares nationally will be found as regular advertisers in most resources. By consulting these periodicals routinely for such information, our readers will be assured of receiving the most current resource names and contact information now and in the future. To seek out various reputable resources that operate within specific areas or individual communities only, a bit of extra sleuthing may be required. Seeking out personal referrals or recommendations from friends or acquaintances (whether for a local or nationally available resource) is among the most reliable ways to locate them.

AMERICAN BUNGALOW
P.O. Box 756
Sierra Madre, CA 91025-0756
(800) 350-3363
www.americanbungalow.com

OLD HOUSE INTERIORS
108 East Main Street
Gloucester, MA 01930
(800) 462-0211
www.oldhouseinteriors.com

OLD HOUSE JOURNAL
1000 Potomac Street NW, Suite 102
Washington, D.C. 20007
(800) 234-3797
www.oldhousejournal.com

PERIOD HOMES
69A Seventh Avenue
Brooklyn, NY 11217
(718) 636-0788
www.period-homes.com

STYLE: 1900
333 North Main Street
Lambertville, NJ 08530
(609) 397-4104
www.style1900.com

THE GAMBLE HOUSE BOOKSTORE
4 Westmoreland Place
Pasadena, CA 91103
(626) 449-4178
www.gamblehouse.org/bookstore/
A comprehensive source for books related to aspects of the Arts and Crafts movement. A mail-order catalog is available by request. Proceeds of these book sales help support the ongoing maintenance of the Gamble House.

Historic House Museums and Related Sites

The following locations appear in this book, and are open to the public as house museums or historic sites. Most house museums have docents or guides on hand to lead public tours, and some may be viewed at the vis-itor's own pace on self-guided tours. Usually, as a con-sequence of limited funding and volunteer staffing, many locations have very limited or irregular days and hours of operation. Some may require advance reserva-tions for all tours. When planning visits for larger groups, it is important to arrange these well in advance, for the available personnel at any given time may be very limited. To avoid disappointment, it is strongly recommended that even the *current* open day(s) and hours of operation of any historic site be confirmed well in advance of planning a visit, as these are subject to change without notice. By special prior arrangement, it may be possible for some locations to be opened to visitors (sometimes for larger groups only) at alternate times. Some of these houses, and/or their grounds,

may be available for rent as venues for special private events. Because such historic sites are sustained mostly through tax-deductible donations from the public, it is important to support them through frequent visits, through membership, and/or by volunteering time, skills, or services. Each a part of America's precious heritage, these sites are always in need of any monetary contributions to help save and maintain them for our future generations.

BEAUPORT (SLEEPER-McCANN HOUSE)
p. 166
75 Eastern Point
Gloucester, MA 01930
(978) 283-0800
www.HistoricNewEngland.org

CRAFTSMAN FARMS p. 30
The Stickley Museum
2352 Route 10 West #5
Morris Plains, New Jersey 07950
(973) 540-1165
www.stickleymuseum.org

F. HOLLAND DAY HOUSE p. 140
c/o Norwood Historical Society
93 Day Street
Norwood, MA 02062
(781) 762-9197
www.norwoodhistoricalsociety.org/day.html

GAMBLE HOUSE p.59
4 Westmoreland Place
Pasadena, CA 91103
(626) 793-3334
www.gamblehouse.org

GLENSHEEN p. 153
3300 London Road
Duluth, MN 55804
(888) 454-4536
www.glensheen.org

HIWAN HOMESTEAD MUSEUM p. 35
4208 South Timbervale Drive
Evergreen, CO 80439
(303) 674-6262

CHIEF HOSA LODGE & CAMPGROUND
p. 32
27661 Genesee Drive
Golden, CO 80401
(303) 526-2666
www.chiefhosa.com

LUMMIS HOUSE (EL ALISAL) p. 124
200 East Avenue 43
Los Angeles, CA 90031
(323) 222-0546
www.socalhistory.org

MARSTON HOUSE p. 54
c/o San Diego Historical Society
3525 Seventh Avenue
San Diego, CA 92103
(619) 298-3142
www.sandiegohistory.org

MOUNT WOODSON CASTLE p. 131
(Amy Strong Castle)
c/o Mount Woodson Golf Club
16422 North Woodson Drive
Ramona, CA 92065
(760) 788-3555
www.mtwoodson.com

PURCELL-CUTTS HOUSE p. 86
2328 Lake Place
Minneapolis, MN 55405
(888) 642-2787 x 6323
www.artsmia.org/unified-vision

RIORDAN MANSION p. 31
Riordan Mansion State Historic Park
409 Riordan Road
Flagstaff, AZ 86001
(928) 779-4395
http://riordanmansion.museum.com

WHITE PINES p. 48
Byrdcliffe Arts Colony
c/o The Woodstock Guild
34 Tinker Street
Woodstock, NY 12498
(845) 679-2079
www.woodstockguild.org

Note: The following three historic sites are neighborhood districts or general areas that contain privately owned houses and other historic buildings of interest. These may be respectfully viewed from a publicly accessible location, such as from a park, the sidewalk, or the street, but are not generally open to the public. Unless under special circumstances, such as a ticketed house tour, lecture, or reception, or by permission granted directly by the owner, the privacy of these properties should be respected.

ARDEN COMMUNITY
(vicinity of Marsh Road, Naamans Creek, Walnut Lane, Lower Lane, Meadow Lane, Pond Road, and Sherwood Road)
Arden, DE
www.ardenclub.com

ROSE VALLEY COMMUNITY
(vicinity of Rose Valley Road and Possum Hollow Road)
Rose Valley, PA
www.rosevalleymuseum.org

ROYCROFT COMMUNITY
(vicinity of Main and South Grove Streets)
c/o Roycroft Campus Corporation
P.O. Box 743
East Aurora, NY 14052
(716) 655-0261
www.roycroftcampus.com

Credits
PHOTO CREDITS
Thanks to Action Photo of Concord, CA. for their expert help with photo processing; Figures 8-9 from the collection of Paul Duchscherer; Figures 1, 37 and 68 appear courtesy of Douglas Keister; Figure 27 appears courtesy of Dover Publications, Inc., with thanks to The Craftsman Farms Foundation, Parsippany, New Jersey; Figures 10-11, 13-14, 15-17, 20–2174, 107, 118, 129, 146 and 179 appear courtesy of Dover Publications, Inc.

MISCELLANEOUS CREDITS
Figures 25-26: Colorist: Susan Moore; kitchen designer by Pappas Design / Mary Jane Pappas; Figures 54-57:

Restoration Contractor: Rob Rehberger / Mr. Maintenance and Repair; Architecture, Interior Design and Restoration Sevices: David Heide, Mark Nelson, Michael Crull, and Brad Belka / David Heide Design Studio; Color Design and Painting: Gordon Deane and Malcolm MacFarlane / Masterstrokes Painting and Design; Wallpaper (in Figure 56): Bradbury & Bradbury Art Wallpapers; Landscape Architect: Mike Allmendinger / Land Elements; Landscape Installation: Dean's Landscaping; Fig. 65: Wallpaper frieze (in library) by Carol Mead Designs. Figures 125-128: Interior design by David E. Berman / Trustworth Studios; Wallpaper friezes (in Figures 125-126): by Trustworth Studios; Custom carpets (in Figures 125-126): by J.R. Burrows and Company; Curtain and pillow fabric (in Figure 128) by J.R. Burrows and Company; Figure 160: Fabrication of Niedecken furniture reproductions by Leo Barton; Figures 161-162: Dining table, chairs, and sideboard reproductions by L. & J.G. Stickley, Inc.

ACKNOWLEDGMENTS

We are grateful for the many people who helped us to make this book project a reality. Mostly due to space limitations, some homes were photographed but could not be included. Following are homeowners, colleagues, friends, and acquaintances who assisted us in a wide variety of ways. We apologize for any inadvertent omissions that may have occurred.

Helen Alexander Estate, American Bungalow / John Brinkman and staff, Ginna and Allan Amis, Terry Anderson, Artistic License, Dianne Ayres and Timothy Hansen / Arts & Crafts Period Textiles, Su Bacon / Historic Lighting and staff, Steve and Susan Ballew / Sacramento Bungalow Heritage Association, Jackie and Maurice Barcos, Steve Bauer / Bradbury & Bradbury Art Wallpapers and staff, Rebecca and Al Barkley, Arlene Baxter and David Mostardi, John Benriter, Lee Biersdorf and Ellyn Hosch, Barbara Bergum, Lucy Berk, Berkeley Architectural Heritage Association / Anthony Bruce, David E. Berman / Trustworth Studios, Rich Bokal, Lock Bounds, Susie Boyle, Bruce Bradbury, Jane Browne and Celeste Rue, Murray Burns, J.R. Burrows & Company / John Burrows and Dan Cooper, Julie and John Casey, Julie Castiglia, Ann and Andre Chaves, Brian Coleman and Howard Cohen, Tim Counts and Mike Lazaretti / Twin Cities Bungalow Club, The Crafted Home / Dee and Steve Ciancio, The Craftsman Farms Foundation, The Craftsman Home / Lee Jester, Holly and David Davis, F. Holland Day House / Norwood Historical Society / Elizabeth McGregor, Susan and Art DeMuro Paul C. Diebold, Riley Doty, Guy Dragon, Leon F. Drozd, R. Geraldine Duchscherer, Kenneth J. Duchscherer, Steven P. and Sandy Wynn Duchscherer, Mark Dymek, Ed and Mary Lu Edick, Theodore Ellison, Barbara and Robert Elsner, Doug Elwood, Dan and Annie Feidt, Sally Fisher, Roger Fong and Erik Kramvik, Pam Frautschi and Richard Ippolito, Gwen Freeman and Andre' Jardini, Kevin Frisch, Candy Galvan, James Galvin, The Gamble House / Edward R. Bosley, Gibbs Smith Publishers / Gibbs Smith, Suzanne Taylor, Christopher Robbins, Madge Baird, and Jennifer Maughan, Glensheen Historic Estate/ Lori Melton and Gabrielle Allen, David Goldberg, Foster Goldstrom, Lisa Goodman, Beverly Kendall Gordon / Fonthill, Diana and Mark Graham, Vicki Granowitz and William Lees, Julie Greenberg, Arno Grether, Jeff Gumpert, Mel and Shirley Gumpert, Carol and Jim Hansen, Cal Harrison and Cal Sims, Theresa and Steve Helmbrecht, Ingrid Helton and Erik Hanson, James Heuer and Robert Mercer, Denise, Keith, and Stephanie Hice, Historic Seattle, Hiwan Homestead Museum / John F. Steinle, Cathy and Steve Hoelter, Chief Hosa Lodge / David E. Peri and Brittany Maynor, Mary Ann Hutchison and Ben Davis, Glen Jarvis / Jarvis Architects, Bruce Johnson, Joy Johnson, Kristi Johnson, Lani and Larry Johnson / The Johnson Partnership, Douglas Keister, Ellen and Harvey Knell, Louise Kodis and David Glass, Lawrence Kreisman and Wayne Dodge, Lance Knox, Craig A. Kuhns, Landmark Painted Design and Restoration /

Debra Ware and Ed Pinson, The Lanterman House / Melissa Patten, Phaedra and Mark Ledbetter, Lamar Lentz, Michelle and Malcolm Liepke, Helen and Stanley Lindwasser, Boice Lydell, Michelle Maas and James Edwards, Ruth Ann Mack, Randell L. Makinson, Mark Mansfield and Juliana Moore, Janet Mark and Terry Geiser, Suzanne and Paul Markham, The Marston House / San Diego Historical Society / Sean Shiraishi, John Martine, Jane E. Marquard, Vonn Marie May, Kelly Sutherlin McCleod, Carol and Robert McCrary, Veronica McGowan, Cynthia Shaw McLaughlin / Historic Boettcher Mansion / Colorado Arts & Crafts Society, Beth Ann and Tommy A. McPherson II, Dean Meredith, Laura Meyers, Kenane and Brendan McDonagh, Brian McNally, Amy Miller, Beth and Zeke Montes, Roger B. Mohling, Mount Woodson Castle / Susan Peterson, Joseph Mross, Marianne Mullerleile, John Nalevanko, Carol O'Connor and Howard Beyer, Old House Interiors / Patricia Poore and staff, Old House Journal / Gordon Bock and staff, Cody and Bruce Oreck, Pasadena Heritage, Karen and Tom Paluch, Period Homes / Clem Labine and staff, Marsha Perloff, Catherine and Louis Phelps, Jen and Dan Philbrook, Mary and Phillip Pierpont, The Pierpont Inn / Cynthia Thompson, Mary and Smith Piper, Pleasant Home / Laura Mercier Thompson, Judith K. Polanich, Frank Pond, Bonnie Poppe, Jane Powell, The Purcell-Cutts House / Jennifer Komar Olivarez, Mark J. Peszco, David Raposa and Ed Trosper, Riordan Mansion / John Schreiber, Michael Davis, and Ellen Bilbrey, Cheryl Robertson, Jennifer and George Rothrock, The Roycroft Inn / Martha B. Augat, Melodie and Chris Rufer, Robert Rust and Pam McClary, Jan Russell, Save Our Heritage Organization / San Diego, Donna and Stephen Schultz, Jeff Scovil, Debbie and Dennis Segers, Marjory H. Sgroi, Phyllis and Thomas Shess, Sandra Simpson, Bruce Smith and Yoshiko Yamamoto / The Arts & Crafts Press, Marcia Smith, Roland Souza, Frances and Gary Spradlin, Debbie and John Stall, Sandra and Michael Starks, Vivian Steblay, David Stowe and Gene Webb, Ray Stubblebine, Style 1900 / David Rago, Marilyn Fish and staff, Pat Suzuki, Marc Tarasuck and Associates, Laurie Taylor / Ivy Hill Interiors, Marty and Ron Thomas, Jeff Tran, Kitty Turgeon, Jenny and John Vetter, Elder and Gladys Vides / Painting Concepts, Mark Wiesner, Kathleen West, West Adams Historical Association, Patty and Brian Westmoreland, Linda and Robert Willett, Jan Winford, Shelley Wingate / Dilbeck Realtors, Gloria and John Woodcock, The Woodstock Guild and Byrdcliffe Arts Colony / Carla Smith and Franne Entelis, Arlene Wright and Derek Vanderlinde, Dr. Robert Von Gunten, Mary Ann and Steve Voorhees, Linda Yeomans / Historic Preservation Planning & Design, Debey Zito and Terry Schmitt. Appreciative thanks to Jeff Weathers, Don Merrill and Fumi Momota, for their ongoing supportiveness, and especially to John Freed, who has always been willing to share his invaluable opinions, energetic guidance, and encouragement. We salute you!